SOCIAL CLASS, LANGUAGE AND EDUCATION

INTERNATIONAL LIBRARY OF SOCIOLOGY

AND SOCIAL RECONSTRUCTION

Founded by Karl Mannheim

Editor W. J. H. Sprott

A catalogue of books available in the INTERNATIONAL LIBRARY OF
SOCIOLOGY AND SOCIAL RECONSTRUCTION and new books in
preparation for the Library will be found at the end of this volume

SOCIAL CLASS, LANGUAGE AND EDUCATION

DENIS LAWTON

LONDON
ROUTLEDGE & KEGAN PAUL

First published in 1968
by Routledge and Kegan Paul Ltd
Broadway House, 68–74 Carter Lane
London, E.C.4
Printed in Great Britain
by Western Printing Services Ltd Bristol
© Denis Lawton 1968
Reprinted 1969
Reprinted 1970
SBN 71000 3490 3

CONTENTS

PREFACE AND ACKNOWLEDGEMENTS

I first became interested in the question of language and social class at my first teaching post in a secondary school. I was teaching English, and it soon became very noticeable that many of the pupils labelled as 'difficult', or even 'ineducable' (although they were in the top 12 per cent of the population as regards intelligence) and who were grouped together in the bottom stream of the third or fourth year had in common not a lack of intelligence but certain social attitudes and linguistic difficulties. I found that my work as a teacher was illuminated by the study of sociology, and in particular by the research of Basil Bernstein. This book is an attempt to analyse the educational implications of language and social class from a theoretical point of view, and also to make some practical suggestions for the attention of educationists. I feel very strongly that this is an area where any attempts to 'reform' teaching methods and curriculum should be based on sound theoretical principles.

I should like to express my thanks to a number of colleagues at the London Institute of Education who have discussed certain aspects of this book with me, and made helpful suggestions: I am particularly grateful to Miss Nancy Martin and Professor Basil Bernstein for letting me take up much more of their time than I could reasonably expect.

I must also thank the Headmasters of the two schools mentioned in Chapter VI, and also the pupils at those schools who uncomplainingly took part in the experiment.

Finally, I am very grateful to Miss Sophie Bowlby who for several months generously acted as unpaid research assistant, and to my wife who has typed and re-typed, read and re-read the many drafts of this book with only an occasional murmur of complaint.

DENIS LAWTON

LIST OF TABLES

I

SOCIAL CLASS AND EDUCATIONAL OPPORTUNITY: THE DEMOGRAPHIC EVIDENCE

In the 1930's Gray and Moshinsky, accepting the principle that educational success ought to be closely related to ability or natural endowment, illustrated inequality of opportunity existing in the educational system simply by referring to the fact that highly intelligent children of working-class parents were severely under-represented in secondary schools and higher education. The problem seen by Gray and Moshinsky (as well as the pre-war Labour Party and the T.U.C.) was simply a question of *access* to particular kinds of educational institutions, grammar schools in particular. It was not until after 1945 that a number of studies took a wider view of the problem. In the post-war years it became clear that *access* to grammar schools was not the only problem: the more subtle questions of *retention* (including the problem of working-class 'early leavers') and differential *performance* have increasingly been regarded as of considerable importance.

Access. There are a number of factors which affect access to selective secondary schools: the size of the eleven-year-old cohort, the supply of places, the social composition of the area and the criteria of selection. All of these factors will interact with social class as an influence. In contrast to the pre-war position, however, by 1956 Mrs. Floud and her associates were able to say that if measured I.Q. were taken as the criterion, the problem of access to grammar schools had been settled by the 1944 Act: according to measured intelligence the working-class pupils were getting their 'fair share' of places in the two areas studied.

Social Class and Educational Opportunity

TABLE 1

Social Origins of Boys Entering Secondary Grammar Schools
Before and After 1944. England and Wales

Occupations of Fathers	1930–41	1946–51
	%	%
Professional and managerial	40	26
Clerical and other non-manual	20	18
Manual	40	56

Source: *Ability and Educational Opportunity*, A. H. Halsey.

In a more recent study Douglas (1964) has shown that over the country *as a whole* there is still a problem of differential access to grammar schools even holding measured ability constant and allowing for regional fluctuations. The working-class pupil at eleven has to be a few I.Q. points higher than a middle-class pupil to gain a grammar school place, for the simple reason that predominantly working-class areas tend to have a lower percentage of grammar school places—lower even than the I.Q. distribution would justify. Douglas also reinforces the argument put forward by Vernon and quoted by Floud that measured I.Q. is not the same as innate ability; Douglas showed that whereas the middle-class I.Q. tended to rise a few points between the ages of eight and eleven the average working-class score dropped slightly between eight and selection for grammar school places.

Nevertheless, so far as access to grammar schools is concerned it is safe to say that the position has much improved since the 1944 Education Act, but there may still be a great deal of wastage of ability at this stage, because differences may exist between innate ability and scores on performance tests. (See Vernon (1955) who stated that measured intelligence was to some extent an acquired characteristic; also the discussion of differences between verbal and non-verbal I.Q. later in this chapter and in Chapter V.)

A system of education which would ensure equality of access to educational institutions would, however, have solved only a part of the problem—probably the easiest part. As was pointed out in the *Early Leaving Report* (1954) still greater difficulties remain: 'From the children of parents at one (social) extreme

2

to the children of unskilled manual workers at the other there is a steady and marked decline in performance at the grammar school, at the length of school life and in academic promise at the time of leaving'.

Retention. The 'Early Leaving' committee, in attempting to explain the difficulties of retaining working-class pupils in grammar schools, concentrated their attention on the pupils' background—mentioning the physical over-crowding of homes, parents' attitudes, and the desire of the pupil to be independent while ignoring almost completely the role of the school in the retaining process: on the question of teachers' attitudes to the pupils for example, the 'Early Leaving' committee stated that they were convinced that no discrimination was being shown, and quoted as evidence the fact that once in the sixth form the working-class pupil was just as likely to become a prefect as a middle-class pupil. A contrary point of view has, however, been put by Himmelweit (1954) who showed that grammar school teachers tended to give working-class pupils lower personality ratings on a whole range of criteria from general behaviour to industriousness. Similarly Halsey and Gardner's work (1953) in four London grammar schools showed that the working-class pupils not only had on the average less favourable academic records than middle-class boys but that they also received lower teacher ratings on personality characteristics associated with school success and were regarded as being less likely to profit from a grammar school education. To what extent the working-class early leaving problem is a question of social background in itself and to what extent it is a question of the power of the school to assimilate such pupils will be considered later. However, evidence has accumulated to show that a considerable amount of human talent has been wasted by the early leaving phenomenon. The Crowther Report (1959) in its examination of National Service recruits showed that there was a very disturbing amount of wasted talent or 'uneducated capacity' especially among the sons of skilled manual workers. Some of this wastage was in the highest ability group but it was especially prevalent in the second ability group. Of these recruits, two-thirds had left school at age fifteen, and only one in four had

3

taken 'O' level examinations. The majority of this 25 per cent had done very well at their 'O' level examinations, and one of the questions asked by the Committee was why the other 75 per cent of this able group were not educated up to the same standard. Working-class early leavers accounted for a great deal of this wastage of ability. In the same ability group (group two) the recruits whose fathers were social class I were three times as likely to become graduates as the lower class boys *of the same ability*. In 1963 the Robbins Report, examining the 'more means worse' argument, produced similar evidence to show that since there were so many high ability pupils (mostly working-class in origin) leaving education at far too early a stage, there was no real danger of a reduction in standards if university places were expanded. The Robbins Committee accordingly recommended a doubling of the university intake by the mid-1970s.

Performance. Although the 'early leaving' problem has diminished to some extent since 1954, there is no evidence that there has been an equivalent reduction in differential performance. The Robbins Committee, taking G.C.E. 'O' level successes as a criterion of performance, compared the figures contained in the *Early Leaving Report* with those for 1960–61 (Robbins Appendix I, Table 14) and showed that it was still the case that a professional worker's child classified at eleven into the lowest third of the ability range was likely to become a better 'O' level candidate than the lower working-class child classified at eleven into the top third of the ability range.

Thus the Reports demonstrated that it would have been 'safer' for a grammar school to select a middle-class marginal pupil than one of the working-class pupils in the high ability range.

The fact that regarding both the question of early leaving and the question of poor performance the school may bear a responsibility as well as the pupils' home background has already been referred to. The studies quoted above would seem to be agreed that the following factors are of importance:

(i) the physical conditions of the home.
(ii) income of the parents.
(iii) age of parents' leaving school.

TABLE 2

*Percentage of Children at maintained grammar schools
achieving 5 or more 'O' levels. England and Wales*

11 + grading	Father's Occupation	Percentage Entrants in 1946 (leaving in 1949/50–53/54) (1)	Leavers in 1960/1 (2)
Upper third	Professional and managerial	80	91
	Clerical	65	79
	Skilled manual	60	77
	Semi- and unskilled	42	49
	ALL children	61	78
Middle third	Professional and managerial	62	68
	Clerical	53	60
	Skilled manual	43	55
	Semi- and unskilled	27	46
	ALL children	43	56
Lower third	Professional and managerial	48	53
	Clerical	36	47
	Skilled manual	33	32
	Semi- and unskilled	20	22
	ALL children	31	36
Transfer from secondary modern school		46	45
ALL groups	Professional and managerial	69	72
	Clerical	54	60
	Skilled manual	46	55
	Semi- and unskilled	29	37
	ALL children	48	55

Source: Robbins Report, Appendix I, Table 14.

(iv) parents' attitudes to education.

(v) the power of the school to assimilate working-class pupils.

(vi) size of family.

The first factor could be treated only by wider schemes of social policy, but meanwhile measures such as the Newsom recommendation for a longer school day, or providing facilities for doing homework in school would perhaps be helpful. The second has been considered to be a fairly simple administrative problem of providing grants etc. The other four factors, however, present much deeper problems of a social psychological nature which will be considered in Chapter II under the general consideration of motivation, culture and educability. A final factor which may well be closely related to the last four is the question of linguistic ability. Floud, Halsey and Martin (1956) mentioned this factor in connection with Nisbet's researches on size of family and I.Q. The Newsom Report focused much greater attention upon this factor, and Crowther (1959) and Ravenette (1963) also reported differences in verbal and non-verbal ability. None of the above studies, however, was able to undertake an investigation of the relationships between social class, linguistic ability and educational attainment. Nevertheless, it is possible that the consequences of the linguistic background may be a key factor in working-class under-achievement. It has an effect not only on performance in I.Q. tests and attainment at 11 +, that is in *access* to grammar schools, but also on *retention* and *performance* by its inter-relation with what has been described as 'motivation'. It is clear that for a number of reasons working-class children tend to be under-achievers. In this respect they are less 'educable' than middle-class children. The studies quoted above have been demographic in character: they have indicated the existence of a problem without proceeding very far in the direction of a solution. The following chapters will examine the inter-related factors which comprise this under-achievement complex, and in particular the relationship between social class and linguistic development.

II

MOTIVATION, SUB-CULTURE AND EDUCABILITY

It was demonstrated in Chapter I that the educational performance of large numbers of working-class pupils is far below their potential ability. Various attempts have been made to account for their low educational achievement: Lewis (1953) reviewed the evidence of a number of observers who referred to the general educational attitude of the lower working class as ranging 'from apathy to truculent resistance'; Burt (1945) has mentioned the importance of the fact that the lower working class consists of groups traditionally outside the educational system—hence their lack of motivation.

To explain differential achievement simply in terms of motivation, however, is completely unsatisfactory, even tautologous. McClelland (1958) has rightly stressed the need for an analysis of the various factors comprising motivation, and has been responsible for a series of interesting studies of motivation which will be examined below.

It is not the intention to make a comprehensive critical survey of the literature on the concept of sub-culture (which has been carried out by Gottlieb and Reeves (1963) and by Downes (1966)), nor of motivation, but simply to examine educational motivation as a sub-cultural variable. For the purpose of this chapter Malinowski's definition of culture will be accepted, namely 'inherited artifacts, goods, technical processes, ideas, habits and values'. Within a general cultural framework, however, there may be significant differences in behaviour between groups within the culture. These differences will be due either to differences in *situation* or to differences in *frame of reference*: i.e. various groups may have to contend with different *problems* because of their relationship with the 'goods' and 'technical

7

processes', or they may *perceive* the problems differently. Either of these two factors or a combination of the two may give rise to conditions which might best be regarded as a sub-culture.

It would, perhaps, be useful at this point to note the classification of sub-cultures by Downes (1966) into:

(a)   those which precede or which are formed *outside* the context of the 'dominant culture' (e.g. immigrant or regional.)

(b)   those which originate within the dominant sub-culture: either

(b) (i) those which emerge in *positive* response to the demands of the social and cultural structures (e.g. occupation or age-group), or

(b) (ii) those emerging in negative response (e.g., delinquent, messianic, political-extremist).

Unless otherwise stated the term sub-culture in this chapter will be used to refer to Downes's category (b) (i).

Sub-cultural differences can thus be examined at a number of different levels. At the most general level an examination can be made of the values and norms of various social groups. Evidence at this level will be briefly examined below. Then the chapter will focus on the particular question of differences in family structure and organization, and upon those child-rearing practices within families which are most likely to influence 'educability', especially questions of social control. Finally the possible existence of social class differences in cognitive style will be closely examined together with the suggestion that this is related to social class differences in language.

1. General: sub-cultural differences in values and norms

Alison Davis (1948) made a strong case for linking education and sub-cultural differences: 'In order to help the child learn the teacher must discover the reference points from which the child starts . . . his cultural environment and his cultural motivation'. Davis defined cultural environment as: 'All behaviour which the human being exhibits in conformity with his family, his play-group, . . . and all his other human groups.'

More recently Josephine Klein (1965) has reviewed, summarized and interpreted much of the evidence relating to

8

different sub-cultures in England. As a result of her extensive survey of the literature she concluded that there were important sub-cultural differences between groups according to their place in the economic and occupational structure. At one extreme in society she described groups labelled 'the deprived'. These sub-cultures had their own values and norms relating not only to family organization and child rearing but also to adolescence, courtship, sexual behaviour and marriage. Insecurity seemed to be the dominant feature of life.

The next group she described was the group termed 'the traditional working-class people', sub-classified into rough and respectable (rather vague concepts but useful at this level of analysis). The important aspect of the norms and values of this group was that they were reinforced by the very traditionalism of the group. The protraction of traditional behaviour was made possible by the comparatively low rate of mobility in and out of the community. In the studies reviewed the general finding seemed to be that the community was inward looking with close-knit networks, clear cut and largely ascribed role expectations, having short-term goals rather than long-term plans, saving 'for a fine rather than a rainy day', seeking advice from kin rather than from 'them' who were regarded with suspicion. The high degree of rigid conformity to traditional patterns of characteristic behaviour of traditional working-class areas was connected with the mental disposition defined as 'cognitive poverty'. In the children this manifested itself in a very low level of imagination and aesthetic appreciation. There was also a mistrust of the unfamiliar and the abstract with a correspondingly low rate of exploratory behaviour and curiosity.

A third broad category of working-class groups was described: those whose style of life was changing—often because of re-housing programmes resulting in significant residential and occupational changes. These changes in style of life were set out by Klein as follows:

1. From a close-knit family network to a more loose-knit one.
2. From a community centred existence to greater individuation.

3. From a community centred existence to a more home centred one.
4. From a community centred existence to greater participation in associational life.
5. From a segregated conjugal role relationship to greater partnership in marriage.
6. From traditional occupational choice to social mobility.
7. From status assent to status dissent.*
8. From ascriptive values to achievement values.
9. From financial stringency to greater affluence.
10. From an emphasis on the bread-winner to an emphasis on the child.

This is a useful list since it brings together the main areas of difference which various empirical studies had found to contrast middle-class and working-class life. Its main short-coming is that it does not attempt to classify these differences in any kind of hierarchical model. Sociological theory would suggest that changes in the work situation would dominate other kinds of change. A second sociological assumption would be that many of these changes would be accounted for in terms of changes in reference group, but an important qualification missing from this outline is that it ignores the important Lockwood and Goldthorpe (1963) distinction between normative and relational class identifications: a family might become normatively 'middle-class' in respect of all ten criteria without being 'relationally' accepted by established middle-class families.

2. Family Structure

Important work in this field has been carried out by Bott (1957) who has suggested that there exists an association between the

* Mogey (1956) describes status-assenters in the following way: 'They are less vocal; they accept the habits, standards, word usages and values typical of their area and their street; they talk little about problems of class conflict, about Trade Unions, work or any other general topic. They are interested in specific people, in the details of daily living, and they make no general observations other than clichés or headlines from recent papers. They are not worried about the future, they make few plans for their children.'

conjugal-role-relationships within a family and the kind of social network the family is part of. Traditional working-class families in socially homogeneous areas tend to be organized so that the roles of husband and wife are segregated—i.e. husband and wife carry out their tasks separately and independently of each other. A strict division of labour operates, so that no discussion of duties is necessary or desirable. Such families were found to have a close-knit network—many of their friends and relatives knew each other. On the other hand middle-class families in less stable areas tended to have a family structure based on a joint conjugal role relationship—i.e. 'partnership' in marriage, with many shared duties and responsibilities. These families were found to belong to loose-knit networks—few of their friends knew or interacted with each other.

Josephine Klein (1965) makes a further point that close-knit families tend to 'status-assent' whereas loose-knit network, joint conjugal role families tend to be 'status-dissenting'. She also associates 'status assent' and cognitive poverty.

Family structure may be concerned also from the strictly objective aspect of size. It is well-known that there is an important correlation between social class and the number of children produced per completed family. Nisbet (1953) demonstrated the cognitive and educational implications of this demographic factor in his investigations of the inverse correlation between intelligence and size of family. He also found that there was a much closer connection between size of family and verbal intelligence than non-verbal ability. Nisbet concluded that the large family was a handicap to verbal development because children learned to use language more effectively from an adult model—especially their mother—than from older siblings; the larger the family the more this would tend to reduce the amount of direct communication of the child with the mother. One important aspect of Nisbet's work was that he stressed that the difference he had found was not simply one of vocabulary but was one of general verbal ability which would produce differences in performance in verbal reasoning tests, and hence by implication of any kind of learning in school involving similar mental processes. An interesting complication to this picture has been provided by Douglas (1964) who showed that middle-class families have a higher family size 'threshold' in this respect: 'The middle-class children do indeed show a less dramatic fall in average test score in passing from those in small families to those in large. It is not until families of four or more children are reached that there is a substantial fall in score and even beyond this size the fall is gradual up to families of eight or more.'

3. Child Rearing

It is quite clear that size of family is only one of the many factors in family structure which is correlated with lower achievement and it is very unlikely to be the crucial one. Quality of inter-action as well as quantity should be examined. It will therefore be necessary to look more deelpy into those aspects of familial organization and behaviour most directly connected with early learning—namely the often unrelated behaviour patterns usually referred to as child rearing practices.

Many writers including Davis (1948) have attempted to show that class differences in feeding and toilet training etc. resulted in important personality differences of educational significance. Davis pointed out that the middle-class child was weaned earlier, fed by schedule and toilet trained earlier. He suggested that this early training in control over basic drives contributed to the middle-class personality's ability to defer gratification and to channel aggression into socially acceptable forms later in life. The applicability of these results has been questioned by Bronfenbrenner (1958) who reviewed and summarized the American literature on child rearing to show that changes occur in social habits in relatively short periods of time so that successive studies appear contradictory. An even more important contribution has been made by Sewell (1961) who, in his review of the evidence on social class, personality and child rearing, thought that too much attention had been paid to class differences in weaning, feeding, toilet-training, etc., which might have little or no connection with personality formation, and that too little attention had been given to differences in punishment patterns, permissiveness for aggression and mother warmth which were more likely to exert a powerful influence on personality. Fortunately, Klein's work does not fall into this trap, and she devotes a great deal of her book to 'cognitive aspects of socialization'. Another interesting and important exception to Sewell's criticism of the child rearing work is Kohn (1959 a, b,). In the first of his articles Kohn set out to ascertain the relation between social class and the means by which parental authority was maintained. The most important difference between middle-class and lower-class parents was that whereas the lower-class parent desired immediate obedience for its own sake, the middle-class parent was concerned that the child should internalize standards of conduct, i.e. the middle-class parents were concerned not merely with the *consequence* of behaviour but also with the *intent*. The goal of the lower-class parents appeared to be concerned with external appearance, respectability and adhering to normative behaviour, whereas the middle-class parents were seen to value 'good character' for its own sake and to be more likely to treat their children as individuals rather than concentrating upon rigid conventionality. In a second paper Kohn examined the values behind the parents' behaviour in more detail; he found that although both classes valued honesty, happiness, considerateness, obedience and dependability, the words had different meanings for the two social groups. For example, the lower-class parent associated 'honesty' with popularity and being happy, whereas the middle-class association was with integrity of character and an inner system of self-control. One class difference which might be very important for education was attitude to curiosity. The higher the mother's status the more likely she was to value curiosity very highly; the lower her status the more likely she would be to value obedience, honesty, neatness and cleanliness.

Klein suggests that the kinds of differences pointed out by Kohn existing among American social groups are also found as social class differences, or differences between one kind of family and another, in this country:

A general distinction may be drawn between discipline whose intention is to control the child's behaviour at that moment, and discipline directed to the development of an approved adult character. The former kind of discipline may be continued in later life by *social control*, congruent with the kind of personality which responds mainly to the approval and disapproval of other people. The offender would feel embarrassment or shame. The latter kind of discipline encourages self-control which again requires a sub-division, to allow for the difference between foresight or *ego-control* largely concerned with the consequences of actions regarded realistically in terms of the logic of a situation, and *conscience* or *super-ego control* which characterizes a personality largely governed by inner considerations of right or wrong and is rather less concerned with other people's view of the matter. The offender would feel not embarrassment or shame, but guilt.

Klein argues that although most adult personalities are affected by all three forms of control they will be affected in varying proportions. She suggests that the varying proportion will be connected with the kind of personality developed by an individual and that this is determined largely by the kind of disciplinary techniques employed by the child's parents. At one extreme there is corporal punishment, then scolding, the withdrawal of privileges, isolation, praise and blame and other verbal techniques. The more traditional the family, the more entrenched in a close-knit network, the more likely it was to use physical rather than psychological verbal forms of discipline; similarly it is interesting to note that Bott found that all five of the couples in her sample with a loose-knit network employed psychological rather than physical punishments.

4. Cognitive Style

In her review of the evidence on sub-cultural differences Josephine Klein suggests a relationship between social control, speech and cognition. She begins by asking the question 'What differences in parental or children's behaviour can be attributed to differences which are reflected in their speech?' She suggests four areas of difference:

1. The ability to abstract in general terms from the concrete actual situation.
2. The ability to perceive the world as an ordered universe in which rational action is rewarded.

3. The ability to plan ahead.
4. The ability to exercise self-control.

Klein links family structure, punishment patterns and cognition by means of Hebb's concept of 'sensory dominance', that is the possibility that behaviour is more likely to be guided by current feelings, wishes, moods and other such relatively less cognitive and more fleeting stimuli and also that the attention is likely to be attracted to the more obvious aspects of the environment.

Klein's argument is that the greater the sensory dominance (which is inversely related to ego-control) the more it is likely that:

> 1. Obscure objects and hidden functions are ignored. 2. Present wishes, needs, moods are given satisfaction over absent, abstract or future wishes, needs, moods. 3. Temporally more remote consequences or present actions are ignored. 4. Logically more remote consequences of present actions are ignored.

Acknowledging her debt to Luria (whose work will be considered in Chapter IV) and to Bernstein (Chapter V) Klein says that:

> The less people talk or think in words about what they are experiencing, the less they are likely to be affected by what is not actually at present part of their experience, and thus the less likely it is that their actions will be affected by the consideration of factors which are obscure, general, abstract, or hidden in the future.

Klein's argument is that because ego-control pre-supposes that people take into account the consequences of their action (foresight), and because foresight depends on the correct perception of the present situation, the ability to perceive obscure aspects or hidden functions is a necessary condition for the development of foresight and time perspective. She argues that 'words are needed to create a conception of an orderly universe in which rationally considered action is more likely to be rewarded than impulsive behaviour. So verbal skills have motivational as well as cognitive implications.'

15

Schneider and Lysgaard (1953) investigated the deferred gratification pattern in terms of impulse following and impulse renouncing. Josephine Klein relates this area of study to the internationalization of rules and standards and to the McClelland (1953) concept of achievement motivation.

The method used by McClelland to establish the existence of an achievement motivation was a projective technique. Pictures were shown to the subjects who were asked to write a story saying who the persons in the pictures were and what was happening. The content of the completed stories was analysed for 'achievement imagery' such as the mention of competition, long-term goals or unique achievements. Those subjects who were scored high on 'achievement imagery' were regarded as possessing a high level of achievement motivation, and in fact these subjects were found to possess a high level of performance on a number of psychological tests, for example solving arithmetic problems in a limited time, and solving anagrams; they also had high aspiration levels and remembered tasks that they had failed to complete.

McClelland claims that his data supports the hypothesis that high achievement motivation develops in cultures and families where there is an emphasis on independent development of the individual. The parents of children with high need for achievement act as if the child exists as an individual worth developing in his own right rather than as a subordinate part of a larger 'solidary' family unit to which he owes loyalty over and above individual interests.

The need for achievement is defined (1961) as a desire to do well, not so much for the sake of social recognition or prestige, but to attain an inner feeling of personal accomplishment. As it stands this is a very strange argument, suggesting that these kinds of individual needs exist in a social vacuum; but presumably the thesis is to be interpreted to mean that those social values acquired in early childhood have been internalized by the individual. The parental behaviour associated with high need for achievement is that mothers should insist on independence and mastery at an early age, they should reward them when they perform well, and be prepared to withhold affection and be critical in the event of a failure. High need for achievement is also associated with the absence of a dominant father. Early training for independence, as defined by McClelland and his associates, was found to be much more characteristic of middle-class than working-class families, and one study by Rosen (1956) found that middle-class children possessed higher achievement motivation than working-class children (unfortunately no attempt was made to control for I.Q. in this study). McClelland and others have also used a variety of methods, for example, sentence completion tests and Rorschach projective techniques to find out whether subjects with high achievement motivation view the world differently from others. Attempts were made to see whether high n achievement subjects were more sensitive to some kinds of stimulation, and to see whether they thought in 'different categories'. One of McClelland's students, Zatkis (1949), also investigated language as a measurement of different 'modes of thought'. Zatkis found a number of differences between high and low n achievement subjects on a small number of linguistic measures.

McClelland in commenting on these results argued that 'language is the best, if not the only, operational way at present of investigating thought patterns'. The studies by McClelland and his associates are of great interest but unfortunately there are a number of criticisms which have to be made about the general thesis. First there is a certain ambiguity in the use of 'achievement motivation'; it is sometimes used to indicate general achievement including academic performance at school, for example, but it also carries the additional, more specific, meaning of entrepreneurial as opposed to bureaucratic achievement. A second objection is that McClelland attempts to explain too much by means of a single factor. High n achievement is obviously not the whole story: for example, middle-class boys tend to be higher scorers on n achievement than working-class or upper-class boys, but the upper-class boys still achieve more education than working-class boys. A third objection is that McClelland's approach is too psychologistic: no explanation is offered in his terms for those low n achievement subjects who succeed at school and in life, and on the other hand those high n achievement scorers who do badly. Because McClelland neglects to take the social structure sufficiently into account his studies are useful sources of supplementary evidence but do not provide total explanations.

Klein on the other hand relates facility for learning not only to the individual's family structure but also to the general sub-culture. She argues that where there is a strongly traditional group ideas are by definition not open to change: they are rigid and unambiguous. In such families there is a mistrust of the abstract and a belief that no amount of talking will do any good. In such sub-cultures talking and thinking tend to be of a stereo-typed, cliché-ridden variety, and discipline tends to be arbitrary rather than logically planned—for example, a child will be punished according to the parent's mood or temporary threshold of tolerance rather than in accordance with a logically formulated set of rules. It is much harder for a child to learn under these conditions. Generalizations are much more difficult to achieve. This kind of arbitary pattern of discipline thus provides not only a link to the belief in luck rather than consistent endeavour, but also to the child's whole attitude to the new and the unfamiliar. He has not been trained to deal with anything but stereotyped situations; he therefore finds them difficult and even unpleasant. His horizons are limited and curiosity may be seen as a vice rather than a virtue.

It is important at this stage to revert to the argument at the beginning of the chapter: sub-cultures arise in response to different problems, to different relationships with the environment. Thus traditional working-class socialization is perfectly adequate for the kinds of occupational roles traditionally their inevitable destiny. In such sub-cultures education is irrelevant to life: in the home/school/work socialization complex it is education which is out of step. Thus apathy to education is a realistic form of behaviour.

In a rapidly changing industrialized society, however, sub-cultural values tend to lag behind changes in the occupational structure, so that unless cultural adjustments can be made, large numbers of children will be socialized for a world that no longer exists.

Today with the increase in prosperity it is misleading to consider the working classes as a homogeneous group. But the more isolated the working-class group the more likely it is that they will have developed distinctive values, norms and forms of control which will tend to persist despite the fact that they have ceased to be functional.

Bernstein's (1964) view of the relation between socialization and sub-culture clarifies the analysis of the problem. Bernstein relates the occupational structure to family role systems, social control and communication. In order to equip its members with its traditional occupational roles, traditional working-class families will tend to be of the type in which status is ascribed, in which social control is executed by means of positional appeals; roles are assigned and rules are communalized. On the other hand in middle-class families status will be more likely to be achieved, social control will be based on personal appeals, roles will be achieved and rules individuated. This analysis will be examined in greater detail and related to communication differences in Chapter V.

Bernstein's theoretical work (on language and role) should therefore be seen against a background of empirical data on social class differences in language which have been accumulating over a large number of years. These studies will be reviewed in the next chapter.

III

EMPIRICAL EVIDENCE
ON THE RELATION BETWEEN
LANGUAGE AND SOCIAL BACKGROUND

In Chapter II reference was made to various studies of language or linguistic development which revealed social class differences in language behaviour. This chapter will examine these studies critically in order to assess the value of the empirical evidence on language and social background. In addition the methods used in those studies will be surveyed and evaluated to see what measures have been employed and found to be useful.

The studies of children's language up to the early 1950s have been reviewed and adequately summarized by McCarthy (1954). It is not intended that this chapter should duplicate the McCarthy article but rather that it should highlight some of the points of particular interest and then review in more detail the literature which has been produced since the article was written by McCarthy.

McCarthy points out that since 1925 there has been a considerable growth of interest in linguistic development, partly because it has been realized that a child's linguistic expression is a valuable guide to his whole psychology. McCarthy summarizes the studies of Bayley (1933), E. A. Davis (1937), Fisher, (1932), Gesell (1925), Shirley (1938), M. E. Smith (1935), Young (1941), Shire (1945), LaBrant (1933), Heider and Heider (1940) and Nice (1933) which establish crude age norms and developmental stages for such criteria as vocabulary growth, length of sentence, use of compound and complex sentence types and usage of various parts of speech. Some of these early investigators, notably La Brant (1933), stressed the use of subordinate clauses as a mark of linguistic 'maturity'; many others focused upon length of sentence as the most reliable index

20

of development (despite the very great difficulty of defining a sentence). McCarthy herself (1930) in a study of the language development of pre-school children, initiated a system of analysis which sub-classified sentences into: incomplete, functionally complete but structurally incomplete, simple, simple plus phrase, compound/complex, elaborated (i.e. a sentence containing two phrases, two clauses or one phrase plus one clause). This method, with slight modifications, was used in many later studies including Day (1932), Davis (1937) and Templin (1957) which will be reviewed below. One study which is relevant to the subject of this thesis, is that of Shire (1945) who found that the 'McCarthy' linguistic measures were useful for predicting success or failure in first grade reading, but that the best measure of lingusitic maturity was the number of elaborate sentences occurring in a sample of fifty responses.

Another useful method of quantifying sentence complexity was developed by Williams (1937) who assigned scores to certain kinds of structure and thus calculated a total score per sample of sentences rather than a series of frequency counts.

Much of the early work on linguistic development consisted of indicating maturity by changes in the proportion of various parts of speech. Young (1941) reviewed the literature on this subject and showed that the use of modifiers, prepositions and connectives mark important stages in development. The dangers of an over-simple interpretation of such data has however been pointed out by Goodenough (1938) who stressed the importance of *situation* as a factor which produced important differences in its own right.

Of more interest than the simple frequency counts of parts of speech are the studies of sentence structure reflected in the occurrence of various grammatical forms. For example the studies of verb forms and tense changes by Lewis (1951), Adams (1938), M. E. Smith (1939) and Ames (1946) are of much greater importance than studies which simply show changes in the percentage of verbs from one stage to another. Provided that the limitations of studies of parts of speech are borne in mind, however, some of them are interesting and of relevance to this study. The examination of pronouns, for example, by Symonds and Daringer (1930) showed that in written work children used a high percentage of pronouns up to the ninth grade, but then the percentage declined as the context of the writing became more impersonal and abstract. Similarly Goodenough (1938), studying the speech of younger children, suggested that a very high percentage of pronouns after age 3½ might be a sign of linguistic immaturity: with an increased vocabulary the child should be enabled to become more specific.

Many early researchers, including McCarthy (1930 and 1954), came to the conclusion that length of sentence or response was the best and most reliable measure of linguistic development. The main difficulty for research workers in this field, however, has been that the average length of response for any given child varies according to the situation. Smith (1935) found that children used longer sentences with adults than with other children, whereas Hahn (1948) found that when children had an audience of other children in a 'show and tell' situation they used longer sentences than when talking to adults. Despite these difficulties it has been found that length of sentence continues to increase in normal children until maturity and is therefore a useful simple method of judging development. Heider and Heider (1940) presented an analysis of the composition of 817 hearing children aged eight to fourteen:

TABLE 3

Analysis of Sentence Length of Hearing Children

Age of child	8	9	10	11	12	13	14
Mean number of words per sentence	10·2	10·9	11·1	11·1	12·8	13·7	13·9

The main criticism of this technique is of course that it is extremely difficult to define a sentence, and LaBrant (1933) and others have preferred to use mean length of clause as a more reliable measure. This does not, however, solve the problem of measuring complexity other than length, and any attempt to measure linguistic development by counting the proportions of modifiers, prepositions, connectives, pronouns etc. is complicated by the fact that these proportions vary according to other factors such as length of utterance and also that at any given age, these proportions will vary according to the situation. This difficulty has been clearly stated by Goodenough (1938) 'too much attention has been paid to the type of grammar analysis used by adults and too little to the developmental changes in conceptual thinking and social drives that lie at the back of the verbal expression'.

Language and environment: institutionalized children

One of the most dramatic examples of environmental influence on language development is institutionalization. Many studies have been made in this field ranging from comparisons of infant crying-time per day (Aldrich, Sung and Knop (1945); Aldrich, Norval and Knop (1946)); studies of the frequency and variety of phonemes uttered by orphanage and 'normal' children (Brodbeck and Irwin (1946), Irwin (1948), Fischelli (1950)); studies of speech sounds, intelligibility of speech, level of language organization of institution children (Goldfarb (1943), (1945), Roudinesco and Appell (1950)) and vocabulary development (Williams and McFarland (1937), Moore, (1947), Kellmer Pringle (1965)); of all these studies, those of Goldfarb were perhaps the most comprehensive: Goldfarb studied the language of children who spent their first three years in an institution, comparing their subsequent development with that of children who had spent this period of time in foster homes. Retests were made when the children were about 3½, again when they were 6 and 8 years old and finally, in adolescence. The children who had spent their first three years in an orphanage were found to be not only retarded on specific language criteria, but also in adolescence had failed to progress beyond very low levels of abstract conceptual activity. Goldfarb concluded from his many years research that 'cultural deprivation' or absence of external stimulation resulted in a 'primitivization' of an individual's behaviour, i.e. that it was less differentiated, showed a greater degree of aimlessness and a preponderance of trial and error, non-reflective activity. The main interest of these studies of institutionalized children is that they indicate that *social* factors, even at a very early age, have a significant and possibly

permanent influence on linguistic and intellectual development. This point will be dealt with from a more theoretical
point of view in Chapter IV.

Twin Studies

An interesting environmental condition which has received
much attention is that of twins, triplets etc. Day (1932) studied
eighty pairs of twins and found that they were retarded on all
the linguistic measures used, as compared with the singletons
studied by McCarthy (1930): for example the mean length of
response for a five-year-old twin was below that of a normal
three-year-old. Day reached the conclusion that these linguistic
differences were due to the unusual social situation of twins (i.e.
that companionship with another child so similar limited
learning and motivation). E. A. Davis (1937) comparing older
twins, singletons and only children (aged five to ten years) also
found that twins were retarded, but that the gap between twins
and singletons tended to narrow when they went to school and
widened their social activities. An interesting and *unexplained*
finding was that the middle-class twins made greater recovery
at school, whereas those lower down the social scale made much
less progress.

Howard (1946) made a similar study of triplets and found
that they were even more retarded than the twins studied by
Davis and Day. Similarly when the Dionne quintuplets were
studied by Blats, Fletcher and Mason (1937) it was found that
the quintuplets were sixteen to eighteen months retarded at age
five.

Luria (whose theoretical contribution will be examined in
Chapter IV) should be mentioned here as one involved with
Yudovitch in the well-known twin study in which it was shown
that these linguistic handicaps could be alleviated by separating
the twins into different play-groups, and that further cognitive
improvements could be made by a special language programme
(Luria and Yudovitch 1959).

Social Class Differences

McCarthy (1954) introduced her general survey of the litera-ture on occupational group differences with this generalization: 'there is considerable evidence in the literature to indicate that there exists a marked relationship between socio-economic status of the family and the child's linguistic development.' Impressionistic accounts of language differences were traced as early as Degerando in 1847 (quoted in Chamberlain (1900)) who stated that rich children understood more words and less actions whereas the poor child understood less words and more actions. Chamberlain also reported a study by Lombroso which compared the vocabulary of fifty well-to-do educated families with that of a hundred poor children. The first of the more rigorous studies was that of Descoeudres (1921) who investi-gated three hundred children at private and state schools and found that the upper-class children were superior on nearly every item of her battery of linguistic tests.

Buhler (1931) showed that poor children were generally retarded in their development but that they were most retarded linguistically. Children from 'better' environments produced meaningful speech at an earlier age, used a larger percentage of two and three word sentences earlier, and were more advanced in their use of syntax, inflection and sentence structure.

Irwin (1948) in his study of the frequency and types of phonemes used in the first two and a half years of life, found that there were no social class differences up to the age of eigh-teen months but that, after that time, i.e. at about the average age for the beginning of true speech, significant differences began to appear.

The studies of McCarthy (1930), Day (1932) and E. A. Davis (1937) consistently showed striking social class differences: middle-class children not only used longer sentences at an earlier age but also more mature sentence forms and questions. Moreover, both McCarthy and Day found that the differences between the social groups tended to increase rather than decrease as the children got older. (This was not, however, confirmed by Davis's study (1937).)

Young (1941) contrasted fee-paying children at a nursery

school with children who attended free because their families were on relief. She found that the regular group made superior scores on all of the linguistic measures used.

These early investigations, although hardly surprising in their results, are valuable in that they provide a background of scientific data. Apart from the fact that they make little or no attempt to explain these socio-economic differences in linguistic development, another shortcoming is that in these studies no attempt was made to match social groups for I.Q. The criticism has accordingly been made by some psychologists that the differences which have been demonstrated might simply be due to the inherited superiority in I.Q. of the children from the upper socio-economic groups. This point has, to some extent, been weakened by the work of Luria (1959) and others, but will be discussed in detail later in this chapter. Other early investigations do make some attempt at constructing useful hypotheses: Bean (1932), for example, suggested that periods of rapid increase in vocabulary coincided with travel. Working with a more general theory, Milner (1951) attempted to show that parent-child interaction was an important factor in linguistic development: using linguistic tests similar to reading readiness tests, she found that the families of high scorers usually had breakfast together and indulged in two-way conversations before, after and during meals, whereas the low scorers had much less conversational interaction with the mother. Mc-Carthy's (1930) work supports the hypothesis that contact with adults is very important: using length of response as a criterion, she found that for children who associated chiefly with adults the median percentile rank was 70; for those who associated chiefly with older children it was 42·5, compared with the age norm of 52·5; similarly, only children were shown to be the most mature in all aspects of language development. To some extent this might be accounted for by the superior intelligence of these families, but McCarthy stressed that the degree of their superiority was far in excess of what would be predicted on the basis of high intelligence, and that the evidence clearly indicated the importance of association with adults.

One of the most interesting studies along these lines was an educational programme reported by Helen Dawe (1942). The aim of the study was to assess the effect of a programme which emphasized language on a group of orphanage children aged three and a half to six whose I.Q.s ranged from 65 to 92. Each child in the experimental group was matched for I.Q., age, sex and vocabulary score with a child in the control group. The control group continued their normal routine for nine months while the experimental group had a total of fifty hours spent on individual and small group training in understanding words and concepts, looking at and discussing pictures, listening to poems and stories and short excursions (i.e. the kind of experience which children from more fortunate environments would have received from their parents). The results of this very short programme were quite dramatic: the average sentence length for the experimental group increased from 5·34 to 6·14 words. Vocabulary scores increased 17·5 points compared with a 10 point increase for the control group, and the average I.Q. rose from 80·6 to 94·8, whereas the control group mean I.Q. fell from 81·5 to 79·5.

In summarizing the evidence on language and social class McCarthy (1954) concluded that the widespread and important differences which had been found might be due to some extent to the more restricted environment of working-class children. In addition the working-class parents were themselves likely to be less developed linguistically and would not only be a less adequate speech model but also would provide less verbal stimulation. She thought that the evidence indicated that parental attitudes towards their children and habits of family life were the really important factors for language development and that they happened to vary with socio-economic class as well.

Since the above view was put forward by McCarthy (1954) none of the subsequent research has produced any contradictory evidence. In 1957 Templin reported on a study of 480 children from age three to eight. The language areas measured were (i) articulation of speech sounds on tests constructed by the author (ii) discrimination of speech sounds also on tests constructed by the author (iii) sentence structure (iv) vocabulary. The purpose of the study was to describe the growth of language from age three to age eight and to investigate the inter-relations of the four aspects. The results of the study included the close correlation of the four measures, the rate of devlopment over five years as well as sex and socio-economic differences. Templin showed that the children from the upper socio-economic groups were consistently and significantly higher scorers than the lower socio-economic children, and that at ages seven and eight the best method of discriminating between the two groups was by sentence complexity. Unfortunately once again no attempt was made to take sub-groups from the two social classes matched for intelligence to see whether any social class differences would emerge even when I.Q. was held constant. However, one of Templin's interesting conclusions was that the children in her sample were more linguistically advanced than the children of the same age in McCarthy's and Davis's groups twenty years before. In her comparison of the results with those of the two earlier studies Templin found that children in the 1950s used fewer one-word, simple or incomplete sentences, but more adverb clauses and complex constructions. Templin attributed this improved rate of growth to differences in parent-child relationships, so that today children are encouraged to ask questions and talk to parents to a far greater extent than twenty years ago. This is an interesting and highly plausible explanation but in view of the Harrell (1957) study, in which he showed the very great differences obtained from one study to another on the kind of criteria mentioned by Templin, a great deal of caution is needed in interpreting such changes.

One of the few recent English studies of children's language has been carried out by Sampson (1956) and (1959) who has followed up the same 25 boys and 25 girls from the age of eighteen months to five years. In her first study of three interviews taken at intervals of six months, the method used was to elicit speech by the McCarthy kind of stimuli, i.e. toys, picture books etc. This speech was evaluated by a number of measures including comprehensibility of response and quality of response assessed by calculating the proportion of sentences and phrases compared with single word utterances. Slight social class differences were found even though the measures were linguistically not very sensitive (being effectively limited to sentence length). A feature of this study of some interest was that an attempt was made to judge the speech environment of the home by assessing the emotional atmosphere, the provision of toys, books etc. and the example and encouragement the child received in response to his speech. Despite the very impressionistic method of assessment and the limited nature of the linguistic measures a correlation of ·547 between speech performance and environment was achieved at the age of thirty months. Sampson's study (1959) of five-year-olds related the child's speech score at thirty months (the Q score) to a number of tests: (i) Goodenough Drawman test (ii) Stanford Binet form L (iii) Watts' vocabulary test for young children (iv) Watts' English Language scale (v) the children wrote their own names. The correlation between the five-year-old children's scores on these tests and the Q score was low but positive and social class differences were preserved. 'A very coherent developmental picture occurred when the results were studied according to the occupational status of the fathers.' It seems most unfortunate therefore, that no non-test speech samples were taken so that a longitudinal study of the children's linguistic development could be maintained.

Perhaps the best recent large-scale study of children's language was directed by Loban (1963). The study is a longitudinal investigation of 338 children from kindergarten to grade 12. The reports published to date cover the first seven years, i.e. 1952 to 1959. The study was designed to examine vocabulary development, oral and written language, proficiency in reading and listening in relation to teachers' judgement of their language skills, home background and I.Q. Each subject was interviewed annually and his speech recorded in a standardized interview, which included first some general questions on games, television etc., and second a discussion of a set of six pictures.

The most important departure in this study was that the method of linguistic analysis employed by nearly all invesitgators from McCarthy (1930) to Templin (1957) has been replaced by a more complete linguistic model and new methods of analysis. Of particular interest is his development of a measure of subordination—the weighted index of subordination—which is much more delicate than the simple measure of subordinate clauses used by McCarthy, or the index devised by La Brant.

(See Chapter VI for a full description of Loban's Weighted Index.) In addition, for two of the subjects (one high scorer and one low scorer) Chomsky's model of transformational grammar was used to indicate linguistic differences, and this system correlated highly with Loban's other measures of linguistic complexity. For many results Loban sub-sampled his subjects into extreme high scorers and low scorers to determine whether there were different patterns of development for the two groups. One of the linguistic areas under examination was that of fluency: those who were rated high on language ability were more 'fluent', and also they used more words each year than the low scorers. The high scorers also possessed a larger, more varied and more accessible vocabulary and showed a steady increase in fluency each year by reducing the frequency and size of mazes (i.e. false starts, repetitions, unfinished utterances etc.). The low group experienced more difficulty in using and controlling syntax, and accordingly their use of mazes was consistently higher. The second area of study was labelled effectiveness and control over language. This section included the ability to use and vary structure, dexterity in varying elements within these structures, competence with reading and writing, coherence through the use of subordination, connectives, control of mazes, spoken style, conventional usage, and ability to express tentative thinking by means of provisional or conditional statements. A general result was that, although the subjects varied little in their use of basic structures, the high scorers used greater variety in the elements within those patterns, and their control over language increased with age so that the initially high group made relatively *more* progress. There were also very interesting specific findings, for example the investigation of tentative expression: 'the child with less power over language appears to be less flexible in his thinking, is not often capable of seeing more than one alternative and apparently summons up all his linguistic resources merely to make a flat, dogmatic statement.' This result will of course be of relevance to the discussion of language and thought in Chapter IV.

Connected with the findings on tentativeness were the results relating to generalization and figurative language in which the low scorers contributed very few examples. One of the measures of complexity used by Loban was a weighted index of subordination which was found to be correlated, not only with chronological age, but also with general language ability: the high scorers used more subordination than the low group, especially adverb clauses, second order subordination, and subordination which included infinitives and verbal phrases. As might be predicted, the low scorers in any case contained a higher percentage of low socio-economic children, but it was found that subordination in particular was closely associated with socio-economic ranking. In addition, the high group were more competent in reading and writing. Two points were of particular interest. Firstly the gap between high and low widened rather than narrowed with each succeeding year. Secondly writing ability was shown to be very closely connected with socio-economic status.*

Strickland's (1962) study was designed primarily to compare children's speech with the structures used in children's reading primers. In order to make this comparison, however, Strickland and her associates studied the patterns of structure of oral language of children in grades 1–6 of elementary schools.

The method of procuring speech in this study differed radically from those using variants of the McCarthy method in that 'children were brought from the classroom to the recording room in groups of two or three' (no attempt seems to have been made to judge whether the size of the group made any difference, as earlier studies have suggested). The children were then stimulated partly by use of toys etc. and partly by interviewer's questions to indulge in what was rather misleadingly called 'spontaneous speech'.

---

* Making particular reference to coherence, subordination, and rigidity of syntax, Loban referred to the work by Bernstein and concluded that 'nothing in the present research with subjects on the west coast of the United States contraverts Bernstein's findings or conclusions. It also seems entirely possible that subjects from the least favoured socio-economic categories can find themselves at a disadvantage in schools where the verbal linguistic skills of the middle class prevail. Such subjects may find themselves increasingly ill at ease and self-conscious to the point of avoiding oral performance. Such avoidance could, in turn, progressively affect performance in the related activities of reading and writing and in the present study could quite logically account for the larger number of mazes among the children in the low sub-group.'

The linguistic analysis employed was of the same order as Loban's but differing slightly in detail. Perhaps a significant contribution is the fact that this study looked at types of complexity other than that of sentence structure. For example some interesting work was done on noun groups, and elaboration by means of adjectives and adverbs. Unfortunately the main focus of interest was on age developmental differences rather than social class. Nevertheless significant differences were found, both on the use of movables and of subordination patterns and overall range of structure between children with parents of different occupational status and education.

Since the early 1960s the accumulating evidence relating to 'Culturally Deprived' children in the U.S.A. has stimulated a number of studies relating linguistics to practical educational problems. One of the first in the field in the U.S.A. was Martin Deutsch. Although the work of Deutsch (1964) and his associates has contributed little to theory, they have investigated and co-ordinated new methods of measurement and have thus provided much additional empirical evidence. In addition they have resources to plan interesting intervention programmes which will be considered in Chapter VII.

Deutsch's verbal survey operated with a core sample of 292 children and an extended population of 2,500 children. The study was unfortunately not longitudinal but focused on negro and white upper and lower socio-economic status children in grades 1 and 5. The aim of the verbal survey was 'to formulate a nomenclature of cognitive abilities, not simply to demonstrate the existence of differences but to define anomalies and orderliness in perceptual, linguistic and conceptual processes and school achievement'. The survey collected data on over a hundred identifiable variables, the main focus being on language as the key to cognitive development and school attainment. Deutsch's work is potentially of very great interest in that it brings together a wide range of conceptual, cognitive and language tests. The language tests are useful in themselves but should not be regarded as a substitute for collecting speech samples. The complete results of the survey are not yet available.

Although a great deal is lost at this stage by being unable to match groups for I.Q., one interesting result is certainly the greater socio-economic differences at grade 5 compared with the social differences at grade 1, referred to by Deutsch as the *'cumulative deficit phenomenon'*, especially on those items involving generalization and conceptualization. Although it is perhaps unfair to criticize results before the survey is completed, it would seem unfortunate that these interesting results cannot be related to the speech structures of the subjects outside the test situations.

To some extent this criticism has been met by a second study by Deutsch (Deutsch, Maliver, Brown and Cherry, 1964) but unfortunately other methodological criticisms must be made of this study also.

The aim of the second study was intended not simply to make comparative analyses of linguistic development, but was concerned with 'communication of information in the elementary school classroom'. Deutsch defined the problem in this way 'language is a central factor in school performance, both in the major inter-personal communication function of language, and in its intra-personal mediational function in problem solving. . . . With the exception of very few children . . . children grow up in a veritable sea of language. Various sub-cultures use language differently with respect to children, however.' Thus the study attempted to survey (a) the language skills of the intellectually normal, but socially disadvantaged child, and (b) the extent to which information is successfully communicated from teachers to pupils of different backgrounds.

The subjects were selected from first and fifth grade pupils from twelve New York schools representing three socio-economic levels, negro and white, male and female pupils. The total sample comprised 167 children. Information was obtained on general intelligence, reading, auditory discrimination and language abilities.

Language Testing

Speech was obtained from the children by presenting them with a clown whose nose lit up when the child talked but went out when talking stopped. For the fifth grade children the technique was changed to a rocket which moved when the child spoke but stopped moving when the child was silent. The linguistic data were scored for six variables.

1. Total verbal output. (Number of words.)
2. The use of nouns, verbs, adjectives, adverbs.
3. Type token ratios.
4. The number of sentence units spoken.
5. The mean length of sentence units.
6. The use of dependent and independent clauses.

The T.V.O. was designed to yield a measure of verbosity. The T.T.R. gave a measure of verbal richness. The distribution of parts of speech and sentence complexity were indicators of the children's mastery of language structure.

The results are interesting and valuable, but two main criticisms of method must be made: 1. The way in which this expressive speech was collected, although ingenious, would not have permitted maximum differentiation. It would tend to encourage a very limited kind of speech, i.e. the well organized utterances requiring very little verbal planning. (Deutsch admits this as a fault when referring to the rocket but was apparently satisfied with the clown technique.) 2. The linguistic measures for this kind of research should have been much more delicate: as many other researchers have pointed out, distribution of parts of speech and simple measures of dependent clauses are inadequate indicators of children's mastery of language structure.

Additionally, tests were made of the extent to which information was successfully communicated from teachers to pupils of various backgrounds, and the close procedure was used for this purpose (using the speech of the tested children's teachers).

Results

1. The range of oral vocabulary tended to be independent of the other language measures which were used and was related to social class. But this relationship was not maintained when differences in I.Q. score were controlled.
2. Mean sentence length was related to social class among the first grade but not among the fifth grade children.

3. Language differences at the fifth grade level were greater than those found at first grade level.

Despite the somewhat inconclusive nature of the results Deutsch concluded that the results suggested that children of different social levels varied more in *how* they expressed themselves than in *how much* they express. He suggested that it was experience that largely determined the child's language development, including his skill in using language for different purposes—the extent to which the child could manipulate ideas (even those ideas which he possessed the language skills to consider) was a function of his background. '. . . the major distinction between the language experience of middle- and lower-class children is the difference in training which their respective cultures offer them in dealing with abstract ideas.'

Deutsch also considered that the results obtained indicated that there was a language barrier between the middle-class teacher and the lower-class child, particularly the child in higher elementary school grades.

Vera John (1962) reported on a more specific study arising out of the Deutsch verbal survey. Two hundred and fifty negro children differing in age and social class were studied in detail. Her intention was not to collect speech samples but to use the findings of previous researchers as a basis for relating verbal behaviour and classification behaviour. At the beginning of her study John made a valid comment on descriptive studies of language development when she said that previous investigations merely pointed out that children from lower-class backgrounds differed in their language from middle-class children, but lacked a unified theoretical approach to language and cognition. Having made this point, Vera John proceeded to delineate three major levels of language behaviour, and although her three levels are open to some criticism, they provide a useful theoretical framework for the tasks she sets herself. The three levels postulated were labelling, relating and categorizing.

1. Labelling was measured by the P.P.V.T. (for receptive vocabulary), by W.I.S.C. vocabulary scale, and by a verbal identification test which was used to study enumerating and integrating behaviour. One hypothesis was that there would be

little socio-economic difference on the enumerating task of the V.I.T. but that differences would be much greater on the more abstract integrating task. This hypothesis was confirmed with the additional finding that differences were greater at grade 5 than at grade 1.

2.   Relating, according to John, is comparable to the linguists' syntactic analysis, and was tested by the word association test. The test was used to see what kind of verbal 'filing system' of word classes was available to the children. John found this test to be a highly sensitive measure of 'language socialization' in that middle-class children were more likely to respond to a highly sensitive measure of 'language socialization' in that middle-class children were more likely to respond to a stimulus word with a word of the same form class, i.e. the middle-class children tended more to approximate the adult pattern of responses than the lower-class children of the same age grade.

3.   Classification was taken to mean the 'language conceptual level' i.e. language to categorize objects, people and events in the environment. This aspect of language was measured by a concept sorting task of sixteen cards which could be grouped into functional pairs (e.g. sailor and boat) or into logically consistent piles of four cards (e.g. means of transport etc.). In addition to sorting the cards, the children were asked to give some kind of verbal justification for their choice. The results of the concept sorting task were that no significant differences were found for first grade children but that, for the fifth grade children, 45 per cent of the middle-class subjects sorted the cards into four concept piles, compared with only 15 per cent of the lower-class fifth grade children. In addition the successful lower-class children gave significantly fewer explicit verbalizations of their sorting behaviour than the middle-class.

John summarizes her results by stating that the middle-class child has a distinct advantage where precise and abstract language is needed and that these social class differences are greater with fifth grade children than with those five years younger.

Despite John's rather facile comparison of her three 'levels', of labelling, relating and categorizing with three linguistic levels of morphology, syntax and 'internal or covert language processes' (a comparison without theoretical or empirical justification) she nevertheless provides results of great practical and theoretical interest.

These studies of Deutsch and his associates, and Vera John, have now brought the methodology a long way from the purely descriptive developmental studies of the 1930s which were reviewed at the beginning of this chapter. In fact they have illustrated the need to consider the theoretical implications of the relation of language and thought which will be the subject of the next chapter.

IV

LANGUAGE AND THOUGHT

From the preceding chapters it would seem evident that differences in social background are related to differences in linguistic development and also that differences in social background are related to educational attainment. One question that remains is whether there is, or to what extent there is, a causal relationship between the use of language and cognitive development. Given extreme cases, for example deaf children, it would seem clear that backwardness or specific handicaps can be directly related to linguistic deficiency; but with less extreme instances it is much more difficult to determine exactly what part language might play in 'educability'. This chapter will begin with an examination of some psychological approaches to the relation between language and cognitive development which are relevant to the thesis discussed in Chapter V; the second part of this chapter will deal with some social anthropological studies on the language-culture controversy.

I. THE PSYCHOLOGICAL APPROACH

A review of all the arguments for and against the identification of language and thought would be inappropriate, since this has been carried out in a number of psychological textbooks, perhaps most thoroughly by Humphrey (1951). It also seems that now most psychologists are agreed that there are forms of thought which are non-verbal but that, without language, thinking is limited. For example Miller (1951) has put forward the view that 'thinking is never more precise than the language it uses'. It is not, therefore, intended that this section should be a comprehensive survey of the psychological literature on the subject, but an attempt will be made to summarize the particu-

38

lar contribution of the Russians—especially Pavlov, Vygotsky and Luria; then the theories of Piaget will be examined insofar as they relate to language and thought, and some brief references will be made to the work of Osgood, Brain, Skinner and Bruner. This 'psychological' section will then conclude with an examination of some of the empirical studies concerned with language and cognitive abilities.

Pavlov

Pavlov is well known in the West for his work on the kind of conditioning he called the first signal system, i.e. how the mass of stimuli from the external world signals its properties to the organism. He has, however, received much less acknowledgement for his extension of this work to human beings: Pavlov's theory (1928, 1941) was that for man *words* also act as stimuli (and not simply as dogs react to verbal commands). Pavlov went further and said that these verbal stimuli are for human beings qualitatively different from those of animals because of the predominant influence of speech—the second signal system.

> When the developing animal world reached the stage of man, an extremely important addition was made to the mechanism of higher nervous activity. In the animal, reality is signalized almost exclusively by stimulations and the traces they make in the cerebral hemispheres which directly lead to the special cells of the visual, auditory or other receptors of the organism. This is what we too possess in the shape of impressions, sensations and ideas of the world around us, both the natural and the social—with the exception of oral and written speech. This is the first system of signals of reality common to man and the animals. But speech constitutes a second system of signals of reality which is peculiarly ours, and is a signal of the first signals. On the one hand the numerous speech stimulations have removed us from reality, on the other, it is precisely speech which has made us human (1941).

An interesting factor arising out of the second signal system in man is that Pavlov thought that although the fundamental laws governing the activity of the first signal system must also govern that of the second signal system, he also stressed that because of the existence of the second signal system the first signal system in man differed from that of animals because there was in man an integral relation between the two systems. It is this unique human ability, according to Palvov, which enables man to attain the highest forms of *conceptual thinking*, by progressing from specific labels to more generalized and abstract levels of language and of thought.

One important aspect of the Pavlov viewpoint for this thesis is the emphasis placed on the role of variety of context and experience in the development of Language and Thought.

Vygotsky

Vygotsky (1962) begins his analysis of 'the genetic roots of thought and speech' by observing that the relation between thought and speech is not constant and that their growth curves do not run parallel but cross and recross. There is in humans both pre-intellectual 'speech' (babbling, etc.) and pre-linguistic thought. In the studies of the anthropoids there was no reason to assume any connection between the 'speech' of the apes and their problem-solving behaviour, but with human beings, although speech and thought developed separately, they became fused at about the age of two years to initiate a new form of behaviour unknown to animals.

Vygotsky traces the development of speech and thought from this point, and finds it necessary to disagree with Piaget's model of primitive autistic thought becoming egocentric speech which eventually fades away at about six or seven years when speech becomes more and more 'socialized'. Vygotsky's investigations led him to believe that speech was essentially social in origin and that egocentric speech was not, as Piaget thought, semi-intelligible utterances spoken on the assumption that it would be understood by those present, but was frequently speech for oneself not merely accompanying certain activities but serving the purpose of self-orientation. This kind of egocentric speech (speech for self) would later develop into silent inner speech and thought, whereas socialized speech developed into speech for others. Vygotsky put forward a series of excellent arguments to support his criticism of Piaget. Firstly he suggested that if ego-centric speech developed into socialized speech then the structural characteristics of egocentric speech should gradually diminish, whereas in fact the opposite is true—the egocentric speech of a three-year-old is more intelligible than that of a seven-year-old. This Vygotsky takes to be support for his view that egocentric speech does not die, but becomes still more abbreviated and more and more different from external speech (speech for others), and eventually becomes inner speech. He suggests the analogy of a child ceasing to count on his fingers, making the point that it would be very wrong to conclude from this disappearance of the outward manifestation that the child from that point in his life onwards no longer indulged in counting behaviour.

Vygotsky provided further supporting evidence by a series of experiments similar to the Piaget egocentric speech situations but with important modifications built in: i.e. he deliberately weakened the social aspects of the relationship by including an 'audience' of deaf or foreign children, or produced so much noise that the 'egocentric' speaker would in any case be inaudible. Under these circumstances the child tended to stop talking altogether or very much reduced his talking. Vygotsky's explanation is that at this stage the child cannot clearly distinguish between speech for self and speech for others and therefore, if the feeling of being understood is removed, then the child will stop talking. Thus the two models could be represented diagrammatically as follows:

Piaget: * autistic speech →egocentric speech →socialized speech
Vygotsky: social origin ⎰ speech for self→inner speech, thought
of speech→ ⎱ external speech→speech for others

Using a slightly different developmental model, Vygotsky sees speech and thought in four phases: (1) the primitive or natural stage of pre-intellectual speech and pre-verbal thought

* By 1962 Piaget had modified his own view '. . . Vygotsky proposed a new hypothesis: that egocentric speech is the point of departure for the development of inner speech, which is found at a later stage of development, and that this interiorized language can serve both autistic and logical thinking. I find myself in complete agreement. . . .'

(2) the naïve psychology stage when the child uses correct grammatical structures without understanding the logical operations of 'if, when, because, etc.', that is Vygotsky agrees with Piaget that the child masters syntax of speech before syntax of thought (3) the external signs and operations stage when the child counts on his fingers and indulges in egocentric speech (4) the ingrowth stage when the child begins to count in his head, use logical memory and inner soundless speech.

Summing up his views on the language-thought relationship Vygotsky states:

> Schematically we may imagine thought and speech as two intersecting circles. In their overlapping parts thought and speech coincide to produce what is called verbal thought. Verbal thought, however, does not by any means include all forms of thought or all forms of speech. There is a vast area of thought that has no direct relation to speech, the thinking manifested in the use of tools belongs in this area as does practical intellect in general. Furthermore investigations by some psychologists of the Wurzburg school have demonstrated that thought can function without any word images or speech movements detectable through self observation. The latest experiments show also that there is no direct correspondence between inner speech and the subject's tongue or larynx movements. Nor are there any psychological reasons to derive all forms of speech activity from thought. No thought process may be involved when a subject silently recites to himself a poem learnt by heart or mentally repeats a sentence supplied to him for experimental purposes, Watson notwithstanding. Finally there is 'lyrical' speech prompted by emotion. Though it has all the earmarks of speech it can scarcely be classified with intellectual activity in the proper sense of the term. We are therefore forced to conclude that fusion of thought and speech in adults as well as in children is a phenomenon limited to a circumscribed area. Non-verbal thought and non-intellectual speech do not participate in this fusion and are affected only indirectly by the processes of verbal thought.

Nevertheless in certain areas of intellectual activity Vygotsky was convinced that in the later development of the child's intellect

> the speech structures mastered by the child become the basic structures of his thinking . . . thought development is determined by language, i.e. by the linguistic tools of thought and by the socio-cultural experience of the child. Essentially the development of inner speech depends on outside factors. . . . The child's intellectual growth is contingent on his mastering the social means of thought, that is language.

Or, later in the same book, 'thought is not merely expressed in words; it comes into existence through them'. Vygotsky proceeds to describe in outline some of the experimental work relating much of the theory to formation of specific concepts observing how primitive 'syncretic' and 'complex' forms of thinking gradually give way in adolescence to true conceptualization by means of generalizing and abstracting.

Unfortunately, Vygotsky tells us very little about the details of the experiments, for example what kind of adolescents were involved, whether there were great individual differences, whether there were some who never graduated from complex or even syncretic forms of thinking. These experiments should clearly be repeated and reported more fully, but what is certainly gained from the book is a clear picture of the importance of language in the higher forms of intellectual activity and above all the importance of the social aspects of communication. 'Thought and language which reflect reality in a way different from that of perception are the key to the nature of human consciousness. Words play a central part, not only in the development of thought, but in the historical growth of consciousness as a whole. A word is a microcosm of human consciousness.'

Luria

In his paper 'The role of language in the formation of temporary connections' (1955) Luria refers back to the second signal system of Pavlov, in particular the abstraction and generalization of innumerable signals, and also the Vygotsky experiment in which the child in a frustration situation (for example when his pencil was hidden or broken) began to speak. Luria declares that

> speech is one of the essential means whereby the child finds his bearings in the external world; it activizes the generalized connections formed in past experience which play a substantial part in the mediated specifically human form of regulation of action. In the early stages of child development, speech is only a means of communication with adults and other children whereby the child masters in a generalized form the experience of other people. Subsequently it becomes also a means whereby he organizes his own experience and regulates his own actions so that the child's activity is mediated through words. The full significance of this fact can only be appreciated in the light of Pavlov's teaching on the interaction of the two signal systems characteristic of human beings.

This idea of speech not only as a means of social communication but as a method of self-regulation is the dominant theme running through all Luria's work.

In his book, written in conjunction with Yudovich (1959), Luria establishes his theoretical attitude to the psychological problem of language and thought perhaps even more clearly than Pavlov or Vygotsky. He sets out his objections to the behaviourist theory on the one hand, and the 'idealistic' approach on the other. The behaviourist model which reduces speech to the level of motor habits is rejected because it is an over-simplified and narrowly mechanistic view of a very complex pattern of behaviour; whereas the idealistic view of language and intellectual development as 'the gradual unfolding of inborn spiritual qualities' is equally unacceptable since it is both metaphysical and not capable of empirical verification. Luria himself regards intellectual development in general and language in particular as resulting from the inter-action of the human organism and its environment. Thus the child develops intellectually, not simply by a process of maturation but by reacting to problems presented by the environment and thus

44

developing more and more complex forms of behaviour. Hence intellectual development for Luria, as for Vygotsky, is essentially social development, and language is not simply one aspect of mental growth but the key to all the others. Luria places the role of language very highly because it is essentially language which distinguishes man from animals, so that an individual is able to acquire the accumulated experience of previous generations. This experience is greater, not only in quantity, but also deeper and more complex than individual experience because by defining connections and relations between objects the adult bestows upon the child new forms of reflections of reality. Moreover, as the child learns to subordinate himself to language, it will begin to act as a regulator of behaviour and give him new forms of attention, memory, imagination, thought and action. The empirical evidence in support of this theory is obtained partly from an experimental study of two five-year-old speech-retarded twins. The twins had slight inherited speech defects but, more importantly, came from a large family with very inadequate play activities, had never heard a story read or had a story told to them. In addition, Luria suggests that the fact that they were twins further reduced their need for communication with others. Luria separated the twins into two different groups in a kindergarten and both twins were tested three months later and again ten months later. Yura, the more retarded twin, began a special language programme after the first three months and differences were recorded in three categories, play, constructive activity and intellectual processes.

(1) *Play*. At the beginning of the study the children possessed only autonomous, largely synpraxic speech, and their play was sub-normal for five-year-old children: they were limited to simple games of the immediate situation, they could not indulge in imitative play or games requiring role-play or fixed rules, they were particularly poor at attaching conditional meanings to objects. This was only possible for them for visually perceived direct action but not for verbal conditions.

(2) *Constructive activity*. At the beginning the twins could scribble but not draw and were not able to give a title to any of their

compositions. They failed to make constructions out of bricks and when asked to make a pattern out of mosaic beads, they simply filled up the whole board: i.e. constructive activity in accordance with a verbally formulated task was beyond the twins, because they were not capable of verbal formulations, and thus could not provide themselves with self-reinforcement during the course of the required activity.

(3) *Intellectual processes*. The twins were particularly retarded in their ability to use abstraction and generalization, their speech was still limited to visual direct activity, their language was too immature to permit mental activity independent of the immediate concrete objects, and they were incapable of tasks involving simple grouping of objects into logical classes.

The following improvements were observed after three months:

(1) *Play*. The twins were using language much more extensively in their play and were able to maintain attention and interest in a single game for much longer periods than before, i.e. they were beginning to detach themselves from the immediate and to subordinate their behaviour to more distant verbal goals (planning was now possible because a time perspective had developed by means of language).

(2) *Constructive activity*. Their paintings, pattern designing and modelling were now accompanied by more speech, and the more labels they used in connection with their models the more accurate and realistic they appeared.

(3) *Intellectual processes*. The twins' increased control over language was accompanied by improvements in cognitive tasks involving abstraction, generalization and classification. After ten months both twins had continued to improve but Yura, who had previously been more retarded than Liosha but had received the special language programme, was now superior in all three areas and had made considerably more progress in the intellectual operations: Yura was now using an objective, verbally regulated system of classification, compared with Liosha's

simple form and colour classification. In addition, Yura, who had previously accepted a subordinate role in play activity, now invariably emerged as the leader and initiator of new games.

From this experiment Luria concluded that the acquisition of a higher order language system produced not only improved communication but also important developments in the structure of intellectual operations.

Unfortunately much of Luria's theoretical work has not been adequately supported by empirical data available in the West, but some of the relevant experiments are briefly reported in *The Role of Speech in the Regulation of Normal and Abnormal Behaviour* (1961). For example one of the few experiments which operates at a level above that of single words is the figure and ground experiment, which demonstrates that by means of speech the child can actively modify the environment that influences him and can adapt his behaviour to the modified influences. Acting on the principle that behaviour is subject to the rule of force, Luria constructs the following experiment. When exposed to coloured circles on different coloured backgrounds, without words a child is subject to the perception of the figure which is dominant over the ground, but by means of speech it is possible to reinforce the weaker element in a complex visual stimulus, that is to make the child focus on the ground rather than on the figure. In this experiment children aged three to four were not able to stabilize their reactions to the ground, but with the growth of speech, children aged five to seven were able to be made to react to the verbal signal rather than to the more powerful visual stimulus. If, however, the pattern of the experiment is changed slightly, so that instead of a coloured circle on a plain background, aeroplanes are used on a coloured background, and if realistic verbal explanations are used, then children can be made to react differently; for example if the researcher instructs 'squeeze with the right hand when you see a red aeroplane on a yellow ground because the aeroplane can fly when it's sunny, when the sun is shining and the sky is yellow, but squeeze with the left hand for a green aeroplane on a grey ground because when it's rainy the plane can't fly and it has to be stopped'. When these verbal explanations were given the three- to four-year old children, who were previously unable to focus on the ground rather than the figure, were now able to react to the colour of the ground rather than the figure when the final picture was shown. Thus speaking to a child can reshape his significant perception of a compound stimulus and modify the rule of force. Luria goes on to demonstrate other aspects of verbal self-regulating activity, for example, he mentions the Liublinskaya experiment in which children aged only twelve to thirteen months were required to select the correct green or red box. The correct box always contained a sweet. When the children knew the name of the colour, not only did they learn three times as quickly, but they also transferred the correct colour choice to other objects. Many other experiments, too complicated for detailed report here (but reported in Simon, 1957 and 1963) support Luria's view that abstracting and generalizing verbal activity is the key to the systematization of experience which plays so vital a part in cognitive activity, and that it is this quality which differentiates not only men and animals, but also normal children from those with various forms of cortical deficiencies. Unfortunately the accounts of the experiments are sketchy and lacking in any kind of statistical evaluation. Replication of these experiments will be essential before any conclusive judgement can be made, but meanwhile Luria's methods and reported results are impressive and others among his Soviet colleagues have reported similar findings.

Other Soviet Psychologists

Much of the published work by other Russian researchers suffers from the same faults as that of Luria. Nevertheless they are extremely interesting and suggestive for further research. For example the work of Liublinskaya (reported in Simon, 1957) investigated the ability of children to abstract the pattern (spots or stripes) from one butterfly and to find another similar butterfly from a number of differently marked specimens. The experimental group were given a verbal label for the differentiating factor but the control group were left to their own resources. Not only were the experimental group more successful in choosing correctly (the control group tended to select simply by colour) but they were also capable of very fine distinctions and also of justifying these choices using other verbal labels they had not been given, i.e. they used not simply the original label but a whole cognitive process of verbal comparisons.

In another set of experiments Liublinskaya illustrated the importance of prepositions and adverbs for cognitive operations.

> The part played by language in the development of children's thinking appears most clearly in the way objects and pheno-mena are reflected in their connections and inter-relations. Special connections can be perceived only by perceptual contemplation, but even so they are only understood when given a verbal designation. The remaining connections are reflected indirectly through speech.

Prepositions and adverbs denoting position and special relation-ships between objects were taught to the experimental group by means of 'didactic games'. The control group had no such instruction. The method consisted of showing four pictures involving special and positional relationships before and after the linguistic training. The results indicated not only an increase by the experimental group in the use of prepositions and adverbs, but also that they began to interpret the whole picture as a complete situation, and began to give it a correct generaliz-ing designation. Liublinskaya draws the following conclusion from this and similar sets of experiments:

> (1) The development of cognitive activity beginning with perception and concluding with abstract thinking, requires familiarity with the mother tongue. The mastery of language appears as a condition of generalized human reflection of objects, their features, activities, and so on. (2) The develop-ment of sense perception is inseparably linked with the development of thinking. The improvement of sensation, per-ception and conception *is* the deepening comprehension of the visually presented phenomenon, object, or whole situa-tion. The more complex the situation as an object of percep-tion, the stronger is the influence of the developing mechan-isms of thinking in re-structuring the child's perceptual knowledge. (3) The mastery of words, signalizing different relations among the phenomena of the objective world, is of

particular significance for the development of perceptual activity. This means that the child must master the grammatical forms for constructing sentences. Expressed in a grammatically correct sentence, the child's thought gradually becomes an increasingly accurate and complete reflection of reality, of all the diverse connections and relations between the objects and phenomena of nature and society.

Similarly Ananiev (1955) in a book on special discrimination (one chapter is reproduced in Simon, 1957) emphasizes the importance of language in perception and cognition.

Language plays an exceptionally important part in differentiation. The expression in words of a generalized knowledge of the objects and relations of the external world assists the development of discrimination. As his vocabulary and mastery of grammatical structure increases, man learns to make fine distinctions between external stimuli which are closely similar in nature and intensity. The sharpening of a child's discriminatory sensitivity is expressed in the development of his powers of observation which is closely connected with the formation of the second signal system as the basis of speech and thinking. In experiments designed to study the process of differentiation the appropriate word not only replaces the stimulus which is being differentiated, but also organizes the whole process. The influence of the second signal system on the first is seen very clearly in the development of discriminatory sensitivity. Shvarts' data show that as children grow older, their discriminatory sensitivity becomes very much sharper (in older children it is much more delicate than in younger) although absolute sensitivity increases less noticeably. The development of discriminatory sensitivity in children is inextricably bound up with improvement in their speech in the course of their education and upbringing.

Unfortunately the details of the relevant evidence are not available but it is clear that the Russians have been working extensively on this problem and have produced results which at this stage seem very impressive. It is not only the Moscow school of Luria and his colleagues who are devoting so much research time to thought and language, however. According to *Recent Soviet Psychology* edited by N. O'Connor (1961) much of the work of the Georgian psychologists since 1923 has been devoted to the psychology of speech and especially to experimental work on speech and thought. R. G. Natadze reviews some of this work, but once again the lack of detailed information on experimental design and on results is frustrating. These Georgian psychologists, approaching the problem from a tradition very different from that of Luria, i.e. the Uznadze set theory, nevertheless reach very similar conclusions. Natadze himself used a concept formation study technique to investigate disturbances of conceptual thought affecting patients with speech disorders of various degrees of severity. The technique involved the distinction between 'common' and 'essential' features in concept formation. From the results obtained it appeared that the chief disturbance consisted of a reduction in the synthetic and integrating function of the thought process, that is a reduced power to generalize.

Using similar techniques Kolbaya (in O'Connor, 1961) examined the ability of deaf mutes to form concepts. According to the author, deaf mutes not possessing normal speech were incapable of developing even simple objective concepts. They were not able to master even a simple classification of typical representatives of birds, mammals and fish. It was not only that they failed to assimilate the essential attributes of objects but failed even on general features of a group of objects.*

Prangishvili's article (in O'Connor 1961) is a more general study of 'the unity of thought and language'. The author considered two kinds of theory to be unsound. Both those which treated the development of thinking as a transition from non-verbal thought forms to a logical verbal process, and those which represented it as a process which changed from a type of thinking which is unrelated to the reflection of reality (super-logical thinking) to logical thought. He attempted to show that the development of thought in the child is possible 'only in the form of verbal thinking'.

Until these studies become available in English translation

* A general discussion of the question of deafness and cognition will be found later in this chapter.

they can be regarded only as interesting indications of theoretical lines of thought, but it is perhaps important to indicate that these studies are the outcome of a long tradition of work in this field and are very much in line with the slighter but more adequately reported British, French and American studies to be considered below.

Piaget

Reference has already been made to Piaget in connection with egocentric speech. This is a question which has aroused much controversy and discussion but it is by no means the most important aspect of Piaget's research. Since many of the later researchers have been directly influenced by Piaget's work, in particular by his *Language and Thought of the Child* (1926) and *The Growth of Logical Thinking* (1958) a brief outline of Piaget's writings on Language and Thought will be given at this point together with a review of some of the criticisms that have been made of the adequacy of Piaget's theories.

Piaget's attitude to the language and thought relation is inextricably bound up with his model of cognitive devlopment. To summarize his theory briefly but adequately is very difficult, but the basis of his model consists of the four major stages of development.

(1) Sensori-motor (zero to two years approximately); (2) Pre-operational (two to seven years approximately); (3) Concrete operations (seven to eleven years approximately); (4) Formal operations (twelve to fifteen years approximately).

(1) *During the sensori-motor stage* the child learns to co-ordinate perceptual and motor functions and to utilize certain elementary schemata for dealing with external objects. The child learns that objects exist even when outside his perceptual field. and he gradually co-ordinates their parts into a whole which is recognizable from different perspectives. This is regarded essentially as the 'pre-symbolic' stage but even so during the second year elementary forms of symbolic behaviour begin to appear (e.g. a child opens and shuts her mouth while 'thinking' about getting a watch chain out of a matchbox). (2) *The pre-operational*

or representational stage is characterized by the beginnings of organized symbolic behaviour—language in particular. The child is now representing the external world by internalizing elementary forms of symbolism but he is completely limited to his own direct immediate experiences and lacks the ability to relate these experiences to similar past or future situations. (3) *The concrete operations stage* is reached at about seven years and the child will by now have enlarged his ability to organize means independently of the immediate goal. He will have acquired the concepts of conservation and reversibility and will have thus extended his use of symbols to assimilate past and present experience to future situations. (4) *The formal operations stage* will involve the development of the ability to use hypothetical reasoning based on the logic of all possible combinations and to perform controlled experimentation.

Unfortunately it is not clear from Piaget's own writing exactly what he considers the function of language to be in this process of cognitive development. Obviously the child may proceed from stage (1) to stage (2) without language, but in stages (3) and (4) language is increasingly important. There are three issues which need clarification therefore. (a) Language as a form of symbolization is clearly important in stage (3) and stage (4), but is it a prerequisite or does it develop easily and naturally once the necessary concept has been formed? (b) to what extent is it possible to pass into the higher forms of cognitive development without language, for example in the case of deaf children? Do languages or varieties within a language differ in their ability to facilitate cognitive development? (i.e. this is one aspect of the language and culture controversy to be considered in Part II of this chapter).

There is far too little evidence on all three problems, and Piaget himself has contributed only to the first issue, and even here his present position is not entirely clear. As was observed earlier in the discussion of Vygotsky and the inner speech/egocentric speech issue, the later writings of Piaget are certainly more inclined to give greater weight both to social activity and to the function of language, but Piaget never in fact moves completely away from what seems to be his early position, i.e. that language is important but not crucial: that language follows cognition rather than precedes it. Hunt (1961), in his extensive review of his work sees Piaget's position in this way. 'Instead of language underlying thought Piaget suggests that language can only occur in organisms which have already developed autonomous central processes which can symbolize actions and events.' This position is in itself, however, not necessarily in conflict with the Russian work if it is merely stating that language is not possible without certain minimum mental abilities, but Piaget seems to go further and suggest that language itself depends on the development of images and thought processes, i.e. the so-called *image primacy hypothesis* in which it is assumed that motor aspects of speech can be acquired only after some development of images or schema, the central processes representing objects and events which develop from repeated encounters with these objects and events. This point is discussed by Flavell (1963). Image primacy is however merely an assumption untested by Piaget and Inhelder, and it is included in the general criticism of Piaget's work both by the Russians and by Carroll (1964) that Piaget made no attempt to see what differences could be made at the stages of development by deliberately 'precocious' teaching programmes. Lewis (1963) considers that it is Piaget's attitude to language which is the weakest part of the theory. In his discussion of language and concrete thinking, Lewis comes to this conclusion:

> no doubt a child's cognitive development owes something to his individual characteristics; something no doubt to the maturation of his latent potentialities; to his immediate and direct experience of the world, to a sharpened awareness of its possibilities. But above all his cognitive powers are awakened and developed by his life with others, his contemporaries, his adult elders and through his constant communication with them.

Osgood

Osgood (1953) has put forward a psychological theory of language behaviour in which he differs considerably from Piaget in his assessment of the role of language in cognitive processes. At the conclusion of his review of the American experimental evidence, he is more in agreement with Lewis and the Russians than with Piaget, stressing that 'internal speech may act as a mediating process in dealing with a given situation'. According to Osgood a person is 'set' by his past experiences to behave in a particular way in a given situation; and this 'setting' process is called a 'schema' or 'mediating reaction'. Internal speech is one kind—and a very important kind—of mediating process. Osgood discusses the nature of verbal mediation in this way: a significate, e.g. an object apple, elicits a complex pattern of behaviour. When some other stimulus, e.g. visual perception of an apple, or auditory perception of the word 'apple', accompanies the significate, it is assumed that this new stimulus becomes conditioned to some distinctive portion of the total object reaction, this portion coming to function in behaviour as a representational mediation process.

> This process is representational because it is part of the very same behaviour that the thing signified produces, hence its symbolic semantic property; it is a mediation process by virtue of the fact that the self-stimulation it produces can become associated with a variety of overt adaptive acts which take account of the thing signified.

Osgood's work supports the view that experience will determine verbal mediation and also that previous language experience will facilitate certain kinds of learning.

Brain

Presenting a view in some respects similar to that of Osgood, Russell Brain (1962), has made some interesting suggestions on the neuro-psychological basis of speech: Brain concentrates on two factors—verbal context (i.e. syntax) and context of interest. Both of these are clearly connected with previous experience, so that speed of encoding and decoding will depend on the relative frequency of occurrence of the relevant syntactic structures in the speech environment on the one hand, and on the ideas and intentions of the speaker on the other hand. Brain's theory is that

> the physiological basis of the recognition of the phoneme, i.e. of the basic element of speech, is an auditory phoneme

schema. This is unconscious, for however a phoneme may be uttered, we identify it at once without any process of conscious comparison with a standard. The schema is therefore a physiological organization placed between incoming auditory pathways and outgoing motor ones, and providing the means by which phonemes are both recognized and reproduced.

Similarly at a higher level of organization the word schema operates. Brain does not in fact mention Scale and Category Grammar (Halliday *et al.*, 1964) but a possible conclusion would be to postulate a group schema, a clause schema and a sentence schema—and it would follow that at each level of abstraction, facility in encoding and decoding would depend upon previous experience, i.e. the frequency with which the various schemata had operated in various combinations.

Skinner

Although this section is not intended to be an exhaustive survey of the literature on the psychology of language, since Skinner's work on language (1957) appears to be an ambitious and comprehensive account of speech processes, some mention must be made of the theory here. Skinner's aim is to make a functional analysis of verbal behaviour, i.e. to attempt to apply to verbal behaviour his theory of learning. For Skinner, language behaviour is an example of learning by operant conditioning. Speech is a motor response the strength of which is determined by the pattern of reinforcements attached to it. Thus requests, demands or commands (mands) tend to be reinforced by satisfaction of needs. Another kind of utterance is termed a '*tact*', which is a response to a situation rather than a response to a need (e.g. 'this apple is red'). It is less easy to see in terms of Skinnerian learning theory why a speaker utters 'tacts' since there is no reinforcement of the kind likely to follow a mand; this is however covered by the theory: whereas a mand produces benefits directly to the speaker, a tact benefits the listener, but because the listener benefits he will pass on some kind of social reward or reinforcement to the speaker. Skinner also deals with the fact that some verbal responses are elicited simply by a verbal situation: children show a tendency to repeat sounds and words for the mere satisfaction of uttering them, and these are called 'echoic responses' by Skinner, and the later similar responses to written language are called 'textual responses'.

There are three possible objections to Skinner's reductionist approach:

1. Many psychologists now believe the causation of behaviour (especially human behaviour) to be much more complicated than was previously thought; and are unwilling to accept reinforcement as the crucial factor.

2. The reduction of speech behaviour to S-R, reinforcement and deprivation is inadequate to explain the facts of speech and language.

3. The terminology ('mand', 'tact' etc.) in fact tells us less about language than the traditional linguistic categories. Skinner's attempt to reduce speech to S-R processes has been severely criticized by, among others, Broadbent (1959) and also by Chomsky (1959).*

For Skinner, speech is a set of symbols built up by imitation and reinforcement. It would seem to follow therefore that speech would have no important influence on thought processes. However, even Skinner was prepared to make the guess that the only differences (apart from enormous differences in complexity), between the behaviour of rats and that of human beings would be found to lie in verbal behaviour. But Skinner's work by being deliberately limited to the study of 'observables' excludes any speculation about the nature of thought. On the other hand, since Skinner's thesis is that stimulation and reinforcement are important factors in speech behaviour, if this very limited assumption were translated into social class terms there would be ample evidence (see Chapter II) to show that different subcultures have very different attitudes towards children's speech

---

* Chomsky's own theory of grammar (1957) has at the time of writing, concentrated on the innate structure of language learning, thus throwing more light on what all language learners have in common rather than individual and cultural differences. Chomsky's work lays stress on the inborn structures which facilitate language learning, but this does take for granted a language environment which would enable inborn structures to produce language learning.

and thus react to it in very different ways. According to Skinner these differences in verbal in-put would produce differences in speech behaviour and presumably speech development. Although Chomsky (1959) criticizes Skinner's thesis as a whole, on this point there could be little disagreement.

Bruner

It would be impossible to conclude this section on language and thought without some kind of reference to the work of Jerome Bruner and his associates at the Harvard Center for Cognitive Studies. One difficulty is that any attempt to summarize this work is bound to be an inadequate interpretation.* Bruner's research in this field is concerned with the problem of cognitive growth—'How human beings increase their mastery in achieving and using knowledge'. Bruner dismisses the question of whether it is more fruitful to think in terms of 'stages' of growth or a continuous process as futile, and prefers to speak of three modes of representation which are successive but overlapping means of coping with experience. At first the child 'knows' the world by the habitual *actions* he uses (the enactive mode); secondly there gradually develops a technique of representation through *imagery* which is to some extent independent of action (the ikonic mode); and finally the method is developed of translating action and image into *language* (the symbolic mode of representation). The extent to which any of these modes of representation is employed by an individual will depend on factors such as age, innate ability, education and cultural or sub-cultural differences. In other words individuals in one social environment may be 'stretched' cognitively much more than individuals elsewhere. Language is a very important factor in this cognitive growth, and in technically advanced countries a high level of 'abstraction' is necessary in order to be able to cope with reality. For Bruner it is formal education which is the vital factor in determining the 'cut-off point' in cognitive development, and part of this education process is the internali-

* Another difficulty is that some of the most recent interesting studies contained in 'Studies in Cognitive Growth' (Bruner *et al.*, 1966) became available too late for detailed treament in this volume.

zation of language which is a prerequisite for certain kinds of abstract logical thought.

Empirical Work

Some of the theoretical approaches of psychologists to the language-thought relationship have been examined in detail despite the unfortunate lack of substantiating evidence. This section will continue with an account of various pieces of research of a much more empirical kind which throw some light directly or indirectly on to the general problem; secondly some studies relating to the cognitive development of deaf children will be reviewed, to see what conclusions have been reached as to the specific cognitive handicaps suffered by those with a markedly inferior control over language.

It would seem reasonable to suppose that if a child has learned a concept verbally (as opposed to mere parroting a verbal definition) he would be able to profit from this concept in a learning situation. A limited number of experiments have been carried out on these lines.

First there are a number of studies which show that the presence of a verbal label facilitates a cognitive task. For example that of Pyles (1932) in which he studied children aged two to seven years and presented them with three different sets of papier mâché shapes. The first were five nonsense shapes unnamed, the second were five nonsense shapes with nonsense names (for example Mobey) and the third were five familiar animals. In each set one shape always held a reward for the child. Success was regarded as a correct choice on four successive occasions. The results of this experiment were that the median number of trials needed were 69 trials for the unnamed nonsense shapes, 37 trials for the named nonsense shapes and only 5 trials to achieve success on the animal shapes. The conclusion reached by Pyles was that the presence of a name facilitated the task.

Similarly Shepard and Schaffer (1956) made a study of whether naming would aid the classification of objects. On this occasion the sample was of twelve-year-old children and the method was to use one hundred geometrical figures (five sets of five triangles, five quadrilaterals, five pentagons and five non-sense figures). The hundred figures were originally arranged in twenty-five sets of four and the task for the children was to pick out the triangles. The result was that those who knew the word for triangle were at an advantage in selecting triangles from the other geometrical figures.

Also in 1956 Spiker, Gerynoy and Shepard divided a group of three- to five-year-old children into those who knew how to say something like 'middle-sized' from those who did not, and it was shown that this capability was correlated with performance in a concept attainment experiment where it was necessary to choose the middle-sized stimulus from sets of three stimuli in which the absolute sizes of the stimuli varied.

Weir and Stephenson (1959) studied the ability of young children to choose correctly-drawn pictures of animals from among a mixture of those with incorrectly drawn pictures. Each age group of children was subdivided into matched groups. One group was told to name the animal before choosing a picture, the other group was told simply to point. At each age from three years old onwards, those who were told to name were more successful in choosing correctly than those who simply pointed, and after the age of five the gap between the namers and the non-namers became wider.

Similarly the study by Kurtz and Hovland (1953) examined the power of a word as a carrier of a sense impression. Two groups of children were involved; the first group were asked to circle on a sheet of paper the words that went with a set of objects being shown; the second group were asked to circle pictures of these objects. One week later the first group were better able to record and recognize the objects they had been shown.

These limited studies are perhaps enough at least to cast some doubt on Piaget's image primacy point of view and are of course in line with the Russian view quoted earlier, for example that of Ananiev: 'the development of discriminatory sensitivity in children is inextricably bound up with improvement in their speech in the course of their upbringing.'

But other studies also show that language facilitates transfer to a new situation, for example the work of Kuenne (1946) who used a sample of forty-four children whose age ranged from two years six months to five years ten months. The method of this experiment consisted of confronting the children with two wooden squares of different sizes, the toy always being placed under the smaller square. In the re-test situation there were two alternatives (a) two squares nearly the same size as the original, i.e. the 'near test' or (b) two squares much smaller than the original squares, i.e. the 'far test'. Note was taken of what speech was used in solving this problem and the children were classified into four groups: (1) those who made no comment on the size; (2) those who commented on the size difference without connecting it with the solution; (3) those who stated the principle of the solution in response to question at the end of the experiment; (4) those who spontaneously gave the principle of solution during the experiment. Groups (1) and (2) were younger (mental age three and four). All children were equally successful on the 'near test' but for the 'far test' those children of mental age three had no successes, whereas the children mental age six were one hundred per cent successful; Kuenne reached the conclusion that without language, transposition* is possible to a situation not very different from a past experience, but that as the difference increases, language becomes more and more necessary, i.e. this is not simply a naming activity but a relational process.

Studies of deaf children

One of the problems suggested in connection with Piaget's theory was the extent to which it is possible to develop concrete and formal mental operations without language, or with reduced control over language. The study of deaf children is one way of looking at this problem except that, with improved teaching, there are now very few deaf children of normal I.Q. who have not developed language up to some kind of proficiency. However, their linguistic powers are at least likely to be retarded, and comparative studies are therefore possible to some extent. The ability of deaf children to develop normal cogtive powers is disputed. Some, for example Carroll (1964), refer

* Transposition—the ability to generalize by applying knowledge gained in one situation to a similar but not identical situation.

to deaf children as an example of the ability to acquire concepts without language. Carroll quotes the work of Oléron in support of this opinion, but whereas the work in France does suggest that deaf children's performance is well above the level of cognitive functioning that can be secured from primates, it does not support the view that deaf children without language can ever reach the standard of hearing children. Oléron (1957) reports a study of deaf children using Kuenne's squares as a transposition test. The children were aged five to seven, and the results of his experiment showed that although the deaf children achieved increasing success with age even when no overt use of language was perceived, the retardation of the deaf compared with normal children progressively increased as the transposition tasks became more complex and the relationships more abstract. The conclusion reached by Oléron was that there was a strong connection between the enunciation of a principle and the performance of a corresponding task. Similarly Chulliat and Oléron (1955) studied deaf children aged five to twelve also on transposition tasks, and the result of this experiment was that the deaf were often hampered in transposition to new tasks by the paucity of their language so that they were unable to organize schemes of past experience. Chulliat and Oléron also commented on the inflexibility of the deaf in dealing with normal situations, their difficulty in organizing data and their predominant tendency to use trial and error techniques with little critical reflection and also a high degree of perseverance. In this study, after reviewing the various factors that might cause this inflexibility Chulliat and Oléron said by far the most important was impairment of language, that it was language which enabled a person to disengage himself from a particular situation so as to reorganize it or see it in relation to other situations. Another study by Vincent (1957) studying deaf and hearing children investigated the multiplicative classification by children aged five to eight. The method was to use three kinds of figures (circles, triangles and squares) in three sizes and three colours. Deaf children, when given tasks of classifying things by more than one criteria, used gestures to symbolize class concepts like blue and yellow, large and small; but deaf children are retarded in their classifying behaviour by more than one year.

Vincent reached the conclusion that this retardation was due to the general poverty of their inner language.

On a specifically Piaget kind of test of serial ordering, Borelli (1951) found that up to the age of six and a half there were no differences between deaf and hearing children on arranging human figures, but that on the more abstract task of serial ordering of sticks, the hearing children were able to succeed by the average age of seven years, whereas the deaf children needed another six months before they were able to cope with this more abstract task.

In England similar differences have been found, for example Kendall (1953) in a study of the 'mental development of young deaf children' reported in Ewing (1957), studied a large number of deaf children under five and found that their free drawing was comparatively immature. Up to the age of three there were no clear differences between the scribbling of deaf and hearing children, but at the age of four to five 90 per cent of the hearing children were making representative drawings compared with only 25 per cent of the deaf children. Kendall also noticed that the deaf were less advanced socially and were less able to deal with novel situations.

In their general study of the psychology of the deaf Heider and Heider (1941) noted that deaf children were deficient in the ability to symbolize the future and therefore were finding it difficult to plan a course of action in dealing with a problem. Heider and Heider also commented on the poverty of role-taking in imaginative play by deaf children.

Summarizing the literature and arguing that every effort should be made to develop language in deaf children Ewing (1957) argues that 'there are indications that subnormal linguistic experience causes a lack of intellectual flexibility'.

In a different context Clarke and Clarke (1958) have noticed the absence of 'accompanying' language in imbecile children when attempting concept formation tasks, and O'Connor and Hermelin (1963), although doubtful as to the exact part played by speech in the thought of imbeciles, say

this absence of the directional function of language has been confirmed in our experiments. The mechanisms of this are obscure and need further investigation. It seems likely that whatever causes this impediment limits imbecile cognitive development. Obviously environmental and educational attempts should be made to improve speech ... without some enlargement of verbal conceptualization the imbecile is unlikely to be much assisted in the use of associative capacity.

No final statement can possibly be made on this question without a great deal of systematic research being completed, but the existing evidence certainly indicates that although deaf children without language can reach the concrete operation stage of Piaget's model, there is no evidence to support the view that they are not severely handicapped compared with hearing children in dealing with abstract propositional cognitive tasks.

II. THE SOCIAL ANTHROPOLOGICAL APPROACH TO THE RELATION BETWEEN LANGUAGE AND LEARNING

Much of the best-known work on language and culture has been concerned with various aspects of the 'linguistic relativity hypothesis'. This particular question will therefore be dealt with first, but, as will appear later in this chapter, the social anthropological evidence includes relevant work on much wider topics.

Linguistic Relativity

There are various degrees of attachment to the linguistic relativity hypothesis, i.e. that the language spoken by an individual will affect his perception of the world and his subsequent behaviour. Relatively mild forms of this view are held by many students of language such as Church (1961) whose attitude is not likely to provoke serious challenge.

All human beings of course grow up in a setting of artifacts, symbols and conventions and presumably because of their biological constitutions, are both less fit for direct adaptation to nature and better equipped for mediated artificial adaptations to a largely artificial environment. Some societies, however, exploit their members' cognitive resources more fully than do others, now in the direction of artistic expression, now in the direction of an elaborate metaphysics, now in the direction of technological advance.

However, more far-reaching claims have been made, for example by von Humboldt, 'Man lives with the world about him exclusively as language presents it'; or by Sapir 'The real world is to a large extent unconsciously built up on the language habits of the group. The worlds in which different societies live are distinct worlds, not merely the same world with different labels attached. We see and hear and otherwise experience very largely as we do because the language habits of our community predispose certain choices of interpretation.' The essentially Sapir-Whorf view was that language is not merely a vehicle for thought but an objective reality which completely interpenetrates experience. Whorf himself said, 'we cut up nature—organize it into concepts—and ascribe significances as we do, largely because of the absolutely obligatory patterns of our language'.

Both Trager (1959) and Fishman (1960) have pointed out the difficulties in proving, disproving or even discussing Whorf intelligently without classifying the essential issues and distinguishing between various levels, and also that trivial claims or refutations may be put forward at one level whilst far more important areas are ignored. Fishman suggests four levels:

(1) linguistic codifiability and cultural reflections;
(2) linguistic codifiability and behavioural concomitants;
(3) linguistic structure and cultural concomitants;
(4) linguistic structure and behavioural concomitants.

Level (1) is essentially lexical. One language has a single word for a concept which in another language may need three or four words, i.e. it is more difficult (but not impossible) to convey certain meanings in some languages, hence the stock examples of the four different words for snow in Eskimo, compared with one in English, and the fact that in Aztec there is only one word for our separate words, cold, ice and snow.

65

Similarly the fact that there is no one-word translation into English of 'gemütlichkeit'. However in a sense these are trivial examples, as is the objection (quoted by Fishman) that the presence of the word 'gemütlich' does not indicate that the Germans are more 'gemütlich'. Neither Whorf nor any of his followers would wish to be identified with that kind of facile correlation. On the other hand Lindeman (1938) (quoted by Fishman) has suggested that there are important differences arising from the fact that the French have one term 'conscience' which is the equivalent of both English words 'conscience' and 'consciousness'. This is an example of what Gastil (1959) calls polysemy. Gastil himself demonstrated that what is easily coded in one language may not be so easily or so accurately expressed in another. Such differences are obviously of a much higher order of importance than the oft-quoted colour coding etc., although they are still lexical rather than structural. There might well be some advantage in elaborating on Fishman's first level by subclassifying the 'untranslatable' concepts into physical and non-physical, since the fact that the Arabs have hundreds of different words for camels, whereas we have one, is trivial, whereas the example of French 'conscience' is not. Gastil makes this point: 'Languages differ as to the presence or absence of the field distinctions which they make. A language may be seen as a limited group of words and forms available for the use of a man thinking or expressing himself in the medium of that language. If he does not have the means to do a certain job of thinking or expressing, that job will not be accomplished as well as if he had such means.'

Level (2). The second level of Fishman's analysis examines the lexical differences and behavioural, i.e., non-linguistic differences. The best documented and most frequently quoted evidence is the Brown and Lenneberg (1954) colour experiments in which it is shown that a culturally encoded (i.e. single word) colour is recognized more easily. Another interesting experiment at this lexical level is the Carroll and Casagrande (1958) experiment in which Hopi speakers classified stimuli differently from English speakers in a way corresponding to the different verb structures of Hopi.

Level (3). Linguistic structure and cultural concomitants. As

Fishman points out it is much more difficult to demonstrate differences at the structural level, but clearly Sapir and Whorf considered this even more important. Thus Chinese, for example, has no singular and plural or relative clauses, whereas other languages have tense systems much 'richer' than English: it is here that it is difficult to establish what the cultural consequences of these linguistic differences might be. Whorf devoted a good deal of time to the study of the Hopi verb and suggested that the lack of tenses in Hopi was related to their cultural *Weltanschauung* of timelessness. Similarly Hoijer, studying the Navaho verb in which the actor-action relationship is expressed as 'getting involved in' rather than 'doing', suggests that this linguistic phenomenon is related to the passive, fatalistic philosophy of the Navaho.

Level (4). Linguistic structure and behaviour. The evidence at this level has so far been provided only by experiment 2 in the Carroll and Casagrande study. Casagrande studied groups of Navaho children living on the Indian reservation. Some of them spoke only Navaho whilst others spoke only English. The Navaho language has the unusual characteristic that verbs of handling, the equivalent of 'to pick up', 'to drop', 'to hold in the hand', require special forms depending on what kind of thing is being handled. There are eleven different forms, one for round objects, one for round thin objects, one for long flexible objects, etc., and the Navaho child has to learn these distinctions in order to speak his language grammatically. Having established that the very young Navaho-speaking children used these verbs grammatically, Casagrande then compared the Navaho- and English-speaking children, matched for age, on a sorting task in which they had to use shape, form or material as a basis for classifying objects. He found that the Navaho-speaking children tended to sort the objects on the basis of form at much young ages than the English-speaking children, i.e. that the Navaho grammar which required the children to pay attention to forms, shapes and materials rather than colour, in fact enabled them to guide their behaviour in a sorting task. However, Carroll and Casagrande also showed that language is not the only factor in producing this kind of sorting behaviour since English-speaking children in Boston performed the task in the same way as the Navaho children, i.e. they too used form, shape and material rather than colour, perhaps because they had had direct experience with toys etc., which made them conscious of these differences to a greater extent than the English-speaking Navaho children. This study would seem to illustrate that language is an important factor but not the all-important factor in this kind of cognitive operation. Hocket (1954) comes to an interesting conclusion, having examined English and Chinese.

> Languages differ not so much as to what can be said in them but rather as to what it is relatively easy to say in them. The history of western logic and science constitutes not so much the story of scholars hemmed in and misled by the nature of their specific languages as the story of a long and fairly successful struggle against inherited linguistic limitations. Where everyday language would not serve, special subsystems (mathematics for example) were devised. However, even Aristotle's development of syllogistic notation carries within itself aspects of Greek language structure. The impact of inherited linguistic pattern on activities is in general least important in the most practical contexts and most important in such purely verbal goings-on as story telling, religion and philosophizing. As a result some types of literature are extremely difficult to translate accurately let alone appealingly.

As Fishman points out, Whorf did not claim that all grammatical structure has cognitive effects. Nevertheless a great deal more evidence will be needed before Whorf's theory can be considered substantiated (if indeed it can be substantiated in its original form) and Fishman's systematization should be helpful in clarifying the various areas for study. However, it is still an inadequate framework mainly because it allows no place for the primary influence of social structure.

A balanced appraisal of the Whorfian view was outlined by Hoijer (1954):

> Far from being simply a technique of communication (langauge) provides for them habitual modes of analysing experience into significant categories. And to the extent that

languages differ markedly from each other, so should we expect to find significant and formidable barriers to cross-cultural communication and understanding.

This paragraph is immediately followed by important qualifications:

> It is, however, easy to exaggerate linguistic differences of this nature and the consequent barriers to intercultural understanding. No culture is wholly isolated, self-contained, and unique. There are important resemblances between all known cultures—resemblances that stem in part from diffusion (itself an evidence of successful intercultural communication) and in part from the fact that all cultures are built around biological, psychological, and social characteristics common to all mankind. The languages of human beings do not so much determine the perceptual and other faculties of their speakers vis-à-vis experience as they influence and direct these faculties into prescribed channels.

Hoijer has also pointed out that certain criticisms of Whorf are invalid since nowhere did Whorf attempt to draw inferences about the 'thought world' of a people simply from the presence or absence of specific grammatical categories. For example the often quoted 'Non-Western' concepts of time and matter among the Hopi are presumed to depend not on any one system, such as tense, but on 'fashions of speaking' which included lexical, morphological and syntactic elements 'and otherwise systematically diverse means co-ordinated in a certain frame of consistency'. This does, of course, make the testing of the Whorfian hypothesis even more difficult. However the major criticism of Whorf that remains is a theoretical rather than a practical one, and one which has been missed by Hoijer, that Whorf ignored the influence of social structure and social change on both language and cultural norms. (See Chapter V for a further discussion of this point.)

Language and Culture

At this stage it may be profitable to examine the wider questions of Language and Culture from the point of view of the social anthropological evidence. Much of this work preceded Whorf's studies but has often tended to be neglected since the arguments have been waged over the particular problems inhering in the 'Whorfian' hypothesis.

Much of the writing on language and thought has been the result of the demolition by linguistic anthropologists of the heresy of early missionaries etc. who spoke continually of 'primitive languages' and 'primitive thinking'. The linguistic anthropologists reacted strongly against this and for a long time they maintained 'parity of prestige' for all languages, i.e. the doctrine that one can say anything in any language. This would seem to be true but what is of interest to anthropology is not what *could* be said but what *is* said. Dell Hymes (1964) has clarified this issue:

> for example the many Yana terms for baskets and acorns by themselves would identify a California Indian tribe, but the many terms having to do with eyes and sight indicate an individual concern, one that so far as I know would not have been predicted and does not depend on environment. (The Yana are not reported to have had more eyes, or kinds of eyes, than other people.) Beyond such subtler differences of foci, peoples may differ in the degree to which they exploit the 'meta-cultural' more strictly referential function of language not only in particular areas but across the board.

Malinowski treats of this problem (1923, 1935) and in his review of M. M. Lewis's early work (1937). Malinowski comments on Max Muller's statement 'no thoughts without words' in this way: 'For the psychologists it was going too far, for obviously symbolic thought without words does occur. Linguistically it did not go far enough, for words mean more than ideas, and in their most important function they are as much a form of human action as any type of bodily behaviour.'

Malinowski then proceeded to ask a question which has been carefully avoided by many linguists ever since: 'Can we treat language as an independent subject or study? . . . or must all study of speaking lead to sociological investigation, to the treatment of linguistics as a branch of the general science of culture?' This led Malinowski on to the concept of context of situation which he discussed in greater detail elsewhere (*The Meaning of Meaning* and *Coral Gardens and Their Magic*, Vol. II). Malinowski (1923) maintains that in a primitive language the meaning of any single word is to a very high degree dependent on its context; this conception of context has to be broadened so that the situation in which words are uttered can never be passed over as irrelevant to the linguistic expression. 'A statement spoken in real life is never detached from the situation in which it has been uttered ... without some imperative stimulus of the moment there can be no spoken statement.' The term context of situation was, of course, used extensively by Firth (see below) but more interestingly Malinowski's concept of 'context of cultural reality' has not been taken up to the same extent by linguists. By the context of cultural reality Malinowski meant 'the material equipment, activities, interests, moral and aesthetic values with which the words are correlated' (1935).

For Malinowski language was, in fact, 'primarily an instrument of action and not a means of telling a tale, of entertaining or instructing from a purely intellectual point of view'. Or again 'ultimately all the meaning of all words is derived from bodily experience'.

The linguist J. R. Firth was in some ways intellectually very close to the work of Malinowski especially in his discussion of context of situation in his paper 'On Sociological Linguistics' (1935).

Every one of us starts life with the two simple roles of sleeping and feeding, but from the time we begin to be socially active at about two months old, we gradually accumulate social roles. Throughout the period of growth we are progressively incorporated into our social organization, and the chief condition and means of that incorporation is learning to say what the other fellow expects us to say under the given circumstances. . . . Speech is not the boundless chaos Johnson thought it was. For most of us the roles and the lines are there, and that being so, the lines can be classified and correlated with the part and also with the epsiodes, scenes and acts. Conversation is much more of a roughly prescribed ritual than most people think. Once someone speaks to you, you are in a relatively determined context and you are not free just to say what you please. We are born individuals. But to satisfy our needs we have to become social persons, and every social person is a bundle of roles or personae, so that the situational and linguistic categories would not be unmanageable.

Despite the sociological and psychological naïvety of much of this expression Firth was certainly advancing towards an identication of speech and social structure, leaving behind the vaguer language and culture connection. His opinion that 'We are born into a vast potential cultural heritage, but we can only hope to succeed to a very small part of the total heritage and then only in stages. There would appear to be a need to emphasize that for each stage of childhood and youth, of each type of child, there are a relevant environment and relevant forms of language' ... is very much in agreement with Malinowski's introduction to *Coral Gardens and Their Magic*, Vol. II. 'Language is intertwined with the education of the young, with social intercourse; with the administration of law, carrying out of ritual, and with all other forms of practical co-operation.'

It is this broader view of the relationship between social structure and language and language development in particular which has been neglected by all but a few of the writers on the language and culture controversy. It is however possible to extrapolate interesting details from the writings of some linguists and anthropologists; for example, Harold C. Conklin in Hymes (1964) quotes the case of sex differences among the Hanunoo: 'There is a noticeable difference in the ready colour vocabulary of men as compared to women. The former excel (in the degree of specification to which they carry out classifications terminologically) in the ranges of reds and greys (animals, hair, feather etc.), the latter in blues (shades of indigo dyed fabrics).' In this case the differences in discrimination were clearly due to the differences in occupational function of the men as compared with the women, i.e. differences in social structure.

A more interesting example is provided by Charles O. Frake, 'The diagnosis of disease among the Subanun of Mindano'. In order to participate in ordinary conversations Frake found it necessary to master the terminology of folk botany and folk medicine, and he discovered that 'Subanum medical law and medical jargon are not esoteric subjects, even a child can distinguish Buni from Buyayag—two fungus skin infections not, to my knowledge, differentiated by Western medical science—and state the reasons for his decision'. Frake implies that the possession of the word facilitates diagnosis in this case, but surely the ability to diagnose is a function not so much of the direct possession of vocabulary but of the social organization of this particular tribe: it would be naïve to say that the child recognizes the disease because he knows the word—a more realistic interpretation would be that he knows the word because the social structure of the Subanum is such that every man is his own doctor and that diagnosis of ailments is a very common topic of familiar conversation.

Dell Hymes takes up this point in his introduction to Part V of his book (1964) 'One would expect a fundamental question of social antrhopology to be: how is a language related to the social structure of the community in which it is spoken?' Hymes suggests that the problem should be considered from two points of view, *speech community* and *speech situation*. He makes the point that although speech community is a fundamental concept for the relation between language, speech and social structure it is more often assumed than analysed. As long as one operates in terms of languages and cultures conceived as isolates, internally discreet, it is common to speak of 'The' language and 'The' culture of 'a' people. The term speech community is then little more than a stylistic alternative for referring to such a unit, implicitly interchangeable in its referent with the others. If the equation of a language, culture and people is not taken for granted, but seen as problematic, the identification of a speech community becomes a serious, empirical and theoretical issue. Particularly is this so if the non-coincidence of language, culture and people is seen, not only as a problem of the occurrence of a definable language or culture *beyond* the limits of a given community, but also as a problem of the co-occurrence of more than one within a given community. (This distinction is, of course, of vital interest in the work of Bernstein to be considered in the next chapter.)

In dealing with the concept of speech situation Hymes points out that although Firth had established the concept of context of situation as a technical term in British linguistics, relatively little had been done to show how to identify, structurally, where one situation ends and another begins. 'Obviously things depend on the situation; but on what does the situation depend? Progress in this regard is as much an ethnographic as a linguistic problem.'

At this stage Hymes returns to the point made earlier in his discussion of 'anything can be said in any language'. He maintains that even in a small and tight-knit hunting or horticultural society, different levels in linguistic competence will be recognized, and differences will exist in levels of usage of the language. 'Just as there are no primitive languages without grammar, so there are no primitive speech communities without socially recognized standards of speech. In short, contrary to views sometimes held, speech variation and evaluation are universal.' In the studies quoted by Hymes however, i.e. Bloomfield's 'Literate and Illiterate Speech' and Stanley Newman's 'Vocabulary Levels: Zuni Sacred and Slang Usage' there is regrettably little connection made between language usage and social structure. John Gumperz on the other hand, in 'Speech Variation and the Study of Indian Civilization', points out that 'linguistic diversity in rural south Asia is relatively greater than in Europe. The local dialects . . . serve as vernaculars for most villagers. There may also be some untouchable groups with distinct vernaculars of their own.' Gumperz also makes the point that educated speakers tend to switch freely from one language to another when discussing urban subjects, often inserting entire English phrases into their Hindi discourse. And also that 'stylistic variation seems least pronounced in the speech of those individuals who tend to their own farms. It is greater with those who have outside economic interests or are active in religion and greatest with those who seem to have political ambitions. This suggests that, as in the case of the talking chiefs of Samoa, ability to manipulate argots might be one of the attributes of leadership in villages in India. The need for command of diverse styles increases as we go up the scale to the sub-regional and regional speech strata.'

This is perhaps the closest parallel to the social class differences which had earlier been suggested by Bernstein. But unfortunately Gumperz does not give a detailed analysis of the factors in the social structure which are directly concerned with the linguistic differences, nor does he examine the cognitive consequences of those linguistic differences. An interesting study which makes some attempt to investigate the cognitive consequences of operating with different language forms is Ferguson's paper on 'Diglossia' (1959). His thesis is that in many speech communities two or more varieties of the same language are used by some speakers under different conditions. A typical example would be of a speaker using a local dialect at home or with friends of the same locality but using the standard language in communicating with speakers of other dialects or on formal occasions. In such a case the local dialect is referred to as 'low' (L) and the standard language is referred to as 'high' (H): 'In the Arab world . . . formal university lectures are given in H but drills, explanations, and section meetings may be in large part conducted in L especially in the natural sciences as opposed to the humanities. Although the teacher's use of L in secondary schools is forbidden by law in some Arab countries, often a considerable part of the teacher's time is taken up with explaining in L the meaning of material in H which has been presented in books or lectures'. It is of further interest that Ferguson makes clear that the most striking differences between H and L lie in grammatical structure rather than in vocabulary.

Looking at language and social structure from a very different point of view, Harry Hoijer in 'Linguistic and Cultural Change' in Hymes (1964), makes an interesting historical point. He compares the rapid rate of social change from Anglo-Saxon to modern times, which was paralleled by radical linguistic changes, with the relative lack of both cultural and linguistic innovation among the Lithuanian-speaking people. This is an interesting suggestion and should perhaps be substantiated by other studies of linguistic and cultural changes in other parts of the world.

The thesis that anything can be said in any language is also criticised by William Bull's review of the Unesco monograph 'The Use of Vernacular Languages in Education' (Hymes,

1964). The Unesco committee had suggested that every pupil should begin his formal education in his mother tongue since there was nothing in the structure of any language to preclude it from becoming a vehicle of modern civilization. Bull attacked this point of view, however, arguing that a great many languages do not have a vocabulary adequate to the needs of higher education. The problem was not, however, one of vocabulary: 'in Egypt the creation by the Royal Academy of some 10,000 technical terms has not brought Arabic to the level necessary for adequate instruction in pure science and medicine'. Bull proceeded to criticize the Unesco committee for neglecting the very great problems of grammatical structure and syntax.

There is perhaps enough evidence to indicate therefore that the emphasis on differences between languages, although interesting in their own right, may prove to be no more than a distraction from the real educational-cultural problem, which is essentially a question of range within a language, or control over the potentialities available in one language: i.e. that restriction in the control over a language involves a restricted view of the universe, a restricted mode of thinking, a restricted ability to benefit from educational processes. This educational problem is of course much more closely linked to the wider problems discussed in this latter part of the chapter and especially to the Firth-Malinowski notion of language and the extension of roles than it was to the narrow view of the Whorfian hypothesis which was discussed earlier in the chapter. The way in which Bernstein developed these socio-linguistic theories and connected them with the psychological theories, especially those of Luria and Vygotsky, will be discussed in Chapter V.

V

A CRITIQUE OF BERNSTEIN'S WORK ON LANGUAGE AND SOCIAL CLASS

Several references have already been made to the work of Bernstein, whose theory provides the immediate starting point for the experimental work of this study contained in the next chapter. It will, therefore, be necessary at this point to examine in detail both Bernstein's theoretical contributions and the evidence so far accumulated. It is always difficult to summarize work of this kind without doing great injustice to the author, and in this case it is perhaps even more difficult since the theory is a complicated one which is already expressed very concisely.

It would also be wrong to give the impression that Bernstein's work is simply concerned with the problem of language and social class. It has far wider implications and is relevant to a number of other topics which are not the concern of this book. It will also become clear in the course of examining these papers that Bernstein at this stage was setting out on an exploratory task and was therefore more interested in providing a general picture within a socio-linguistic framework rather than setting down a precise plan of the exact differences between the language of one social group and another. This chapter will, therefore, provide only a limited view of Bernstein's work: in particular detailed work has recently been done on types of family and systems of social control which will eventually provide a much better instrument than the social class setting discussed in this chapter. It is also hoped that this chapter will have some value in its own right since Bernstein himself has never attempted to integrate the earlier and later Papers and to show the development of the socio-linguistic theory.

This review will divide Bernstein's work roughly into three

sections: (1) the early theoretical papers (1958, 1959, 1961 a and b), (2) the report of experimental evidence (1960, 1962 a and b), (3) later theoretical work developing and modifying basic theory (1964, 1965). This list is not exhaustive but is sufficient for the purposes of this chapter.

The first paper will be considered in detail to establish the basic outline of the theory; later papers will be referred to only in so far as they modify, develop or substantiate the work of the first paper.

I. THEORETICAL WORK

Paper 1. 'Some sociological determinants of perception. An inquiry into sub-cultural differences' (1958)

This first study was primarily concerned with 'the gap in the existing knowledge of the relations between social class and educational attainment', and the specific aim of the paper was 'to indicate a relation between the mode of cognitive expression and certain social classes'. Bernstein distinguished the modes of cognitive expression by postulating two types of 'ordering of relationships'—that arising out of sensitivity to the *content* of objects and secondly, that arising out of sensitivity to the *structure* of objects. These two 'predispositions to perceive' were seen as stages on a continuum rather than dichotomies, and Bernstein proposed to analyse them in relation to their sociological determinants and their educational implications. Thus the model at this stage seemed to be:

(1)   Sociological determinants
       (i.e. w-class/m-class environment)
       ↓
(2)   Mode of cognitive expression
       ↓
(3)   Educational performance

The typical lower working-class environment produced a resistance to formal education which might be expressed by (a) indiscipline (b) non-acceptance of teachers' values (c) failure to extend vocabulary (d) preference for descriptive rather than analytical cognitive processes. This resistance, according to

78

Bernstein was a function of 'a mode of perceiving and feeling characterized by a sensitivity to the *content* rather than to the *structure* of objects', i.e. that for the two social groups 'their perception is of a qualitatively different order'.

Sensitivity to structure was defined as a function of learned ability to respond to an object perceived and defined in terms of a matrix of relationships. On the other hand sensitivity to content was defined as a function of learned ability to respond to the boundaries of an object rather than to the matrix of relationships and inter-relationships in which it stands with other objects. The lower working-class and the middle-class groups were regarded as fundamentally distinct because the middle-class possessed a kind of Weberian rationality which expressed itself in the following ways: '(a) an awareness of the importance between means and long-term ends cognitively and affectually regarded, (b) a discipline to orient behaviour to certain values but with a premium on individual differentiation within them, (c) the ability to adopt appropriate measures to implement the attainment of distant ends by a purposeful means/end chain.' Middle-class children were further distinguished by the following characteristics:

1. Children in the middle-class and associative levels were within a formally articulated structure.
2. Present decisions affecting the growing child were governed by their efficacy in attaining distant ends.
3. Behaviour was modified by and oriented to an explicit set of goals and values.
4. There was a stable set of rewards and punishments.
5. The future was conceived of in direct relation to the educational life of the child.
6. The child grew up in an ordered rational structure.
7. Direct expressions of feeling, especially hostility, were discouraged.
8. Value was placed on verbalization of feeling.

At this point Bernstein makes a fairly extreme statement, 'language exists in relation to a desire to express and communicate; consequently the mode of a language structure—the way in which words and sentence are related—reflects a particular form of the structuring of feeling and so the very means of inter-action and response to the environment'. This statement is then supported by a quotation from Sapir, which ends in this way, 'language forms predetermine for us certain modes of observation and interpretation'. Bernstein suggests that these different language forms constitute more than dialect differences because the middle-class family recognizes and responds to a child as an individual and makes use of language structure to express this individuation, i.e. by using personal qualifications the mother at once makes these qualifications relevant to the child and pro-vides a model for the child to imitate. In addition the child's own personal statements will be reinforced and elaborated on by the mother. These different forms of language are described and designated '*public*' (later called *restricted code*) which both the working-class and the middle-class use, and '*formal*' (later called *elaborated code*) the use of which tends to be confined to the middle-class. The utterances in a public language will tend to contain a high proportion of short commands, simple statements and questions where the symbolism is descriptive, tangible, concrete, visual and of a low order of logical implications.

The formal language, on the other hand, was described as rich in personal, individual qualifications and its form implied sets of advanced logical operations; non-verbal (later termed extra-verbal) means of expression took second place. Bernstein emphasizes that it is sensitivity to this form of language rather than extensive vocabulary which is important and which develops into an inclination to verbalize an awareness of separateness and difference.

In a discussion of the middle-class controlled environment in which the 'space, time and social relationship are explicitly regulated' Bernstein states, 'here the critical factor is the mode of the relationship and this is a function of his sensitivity to structure. A dynamic interaction is set up: the pressure to ver-balize feelings in a personally qualified way, the implications of the language learnt, combine to decide the nature of the cues to which he will respond—structural ones.' This for the middle-class child becomes part of his socialization process and deter-mines the level of conceptualization possible.

This now provides the link with education: for the middle-class child, the school, which links the present to a distant future, does not clash with values of the home. Moreover the child's level of curiosity is high and his ability to switch from public to formal language (restricted code to elaborated code) gives him sensitivity to role and status and enables him to behave appropriately in a wide range of social circumstances.

The working-class child on the other hand comes from a less-formally organized family structure with a less clear view of the universe in terms of space and time. Authority will often appear arbitrary; long-term goals are less likely than immediate gratification because the general notion of the future is vague—dominated by 'chance' rather than planning. This environment thus 'limits the perception of the developing child of and in time'. The language between the mother and child is 'public'—containing few personal qualifications and employing concrete symbolism. This tends to limit the verbal expression of feeling, and the emotional and cognitive differentiation of the working-class child is less developed, so that the child will be sensitive to the content of objects because his limited language 'precludes the structure of objects as major referent points'.

This difference between structure and content was seen by Bernstein as 'degrees within a conceptual hierarchy'. Sensitivity to content implies that 'only the simplest logical implications or boundaries of the structure will be cognized. More definitely certain aspects of an object will not register as meaningful cues; or if they do the verbal response will be inadequately determined.' One of the consequences of growing up in this kind of (working-class) environment is that it produces a descriptive cognitive process in which events are seen as isolated incidents rather than being integrated into a logical pattern, and this is clearly connected with the question of curiosity level mentioned above. The working-class environment is thus in conflict with formal education in the following ways:

1. There is a clash between the child's accustomed immediate responses and the 'mediate' responses required by the school.
2. There will be an inability to communicate with the teacher on the teacher's own level.

3. An inability to use language appropriate to the situation of inequality of status between pupil and teacher.

4. The working-class child will resist extensions to his vocabulary and resist efforts to 'improve' his control over language.

5. He will experience difficulty in dealing with more abstract concepts in mathematics and other subjects.

6. This low level of curiosity and his tendency to detailed description rather than abstract analysis will be interpreted as poor application to work.

7. He will have little opportunity to enhance his self-respect.

Comment

This first paper was extremely illuminating in going some way to filling the gap in existing knowledge, i.e. in providing a unified theory to account for some of the socio-cultural causes of poor educational performance. There are however certain difficulties unresolved by the paper and thus possible criticisms of this first presentation of the theory.

(1) Social class is not defined in a completely satisfactory way in this paper. The criteria given for the very vague phrase 'middle-class and associative levels' are educational for father and education or occupation for mother. It is not clear in this Paper whether it was suggested that these criteria were pre-requisites or whether all families which qualified in this way were in the 'sensitive to structure' group. If the former were intended, the argument is rather circular because the middle-class are being defined as those who possess sensitivity to structure, but at the same time one of the descriptive attributes stated to emerge from this kind of middle-class culture is 'sensitivity to structure'. This is perhaps not so much a criticism of the theory as a suggestion that working-class and middle-class are concepts with limited applicability for predictive purposes of this kind, but had to be used for want of more useful criteria. Although it is not completely clear in the Paper, what would seem to be intended by Bernstein is a discussion of three social groups: non-transitional working-class, transitional working-class and

middle-class. These three groups would then seem to be defined in the following ways:

1. Non-transitional working-class. The *father* will be in a manual occupation and possess the following characteristics:

1. No experience of selective education.
2. No specific skilled occupational training.

The *mother* will have:

1. No experience of selective education.
2. No specific training for skilled occupation.
3. No experience of a non-manual occupation.
   She would not have worked in an occupation above that of the lower levels of distribution trades.

2. Transitional Working-class. The *father* will be in a manual occupation and will possess the following characteristics:

1. Some experience of selective education or
2. Some certified training for a skill.

Or the *mother* will have:

1. Some experience of selective education or
2. Have been employed in an occupation superior to that of the father, i.e. some kind of non-manual occupation.

3. Middle Class. Conventionally defined in terms of non-manual occupation and selective secondary education. The implication would be that whereas the non-transitional working-class show resistance to formal education, and the middle-class a high degree of orientation to education, the transitional working-class is in an intermediate position educationally. It would seem, therefore, that in this paper an 'assimilation' view of social class rather than a 'convergence' model is postulated, i.e. the transitional working-class are moving towards middle-class norms at least in respect of education.

(2) The two modes of perception—sensitivity to structure or sensitivity to content—are defined in such a way as to make them inadequate concepts. It is understandable that Bernstein should wish to avoid such terms as concrete and abstract, but

the contrast between content and structure is perhaps both too vague and too specific: too vague in the sense of being very difficult to demonstrate empirically; too specific in as much as it might be thought that other factors were involved in the differences in cognitive expression as well as the content/structure distinction.

(3) In this paper Bernstein acknowledges the influence of Sapir and Whorf but does not make clear his own intellectual stance to the Whorfian hypothesis. In fact the impression appears to be given that the theory at this stage was much more 'linguistically determined' than the later papers (especially 1965) indicate.

Paper 2. 'Public language: Some Sociological Implications of a Linguistic Form' (1959)

This paper sets out in greater detail the differences between public and formal language. The characteristics of public language were listed under ten headings:

1. Short, grammatically simple, often unfinished sentences, a poor syntactical construction with a verbal form stressing the active mood.
2. Simple and repetitive use of conjunctions (so, then, and, because).
3. Frequent use of short commands and questions.
4. Rigid and limited use of adjectives and adverbs.
5. Infrequent use of impersonal pronouns as subjects (one, it).
6. Statements formulated as implicit questions which set up a sympathetic circularity, e.g. 'Just fancy?', 'It's only natural, isn't it?', 'I wouldn't have believed it'.
7. A statement of fact is often used as both a reason and a conclusion, or more accurately, the reason and conclusion are confounded to produce a categoric statement, e.g. 'Do as I tell you', 'Hold on tight', 'You're not going out', 'Lay off that'.
8. Individual selection from a group of idiomatic phrases will frequently be found.
9. Symbolism is of a low order of generality.
10. The individual qualification is implicit in the sentence

structure, therefore it is a language of implicit meaning. It is believed that this fact determines the form of the language.

Contrasted with the public language, the characteristics of the formal language were:

1. Accurate grammatical order and syntax regulate what is said.
2. Logical modifications and stress are mediated through a grammatically complex sentence construction, especially through the use of a range of conjunctions and relative clauses.
3. Frequent use of prepositions which indicate logical relationships as well as prepositions which indicate temporal and spatial continguity.
4. Frequent use of impersonal pronouns, 'it', 'one'.
5. A discriminative selection from a range of adjectives and adverbs.
6. Individual qualification is verbally mediated through the structure and relationships within and between sentences. That is, it is explicit.
7. Expressive symbolism conditioned by this linguistic form distributes affectual support rather than logical meaning to what is said.
8. A language use which points to the possibilities inherent in a complex conceptual hierarchy for the organizing of experience.

In commenting on the characteristics of a public language (later, restricted code) Bernstein clears up one of the comments I made on his first paper. 'The use of a public language is most probably a function of a particular social structure.' This shows that, unlike Whorf, Bernstein regards social structure rather than language to be the primary force.

> Language is considered one of the most important means of initiating, synthesizing and *reinforcing* ways of thinking, feeling and behaviour which are functionally related to the social group. It does not of itself prevent the expression of specific ideas or confine the individual to a given level of conceptualization, but certain ideas and generalizations are facilitated rather than others, that is, the language use facilitates development in a particular direction rather than inhibiting all other possible directions.

In addition, at this point Bernstein makes the very important point, that what distinguishes a middle-class child from a working-class child will not merely be size of vocabulary, but sensitivity to a way of organizing and responding to experience. It is worth stressing this point since so many studies have assumed that providing the right vocabulary would solve the linguistic problem.

Bernstein, commenting on points 1 to 4 of the public language, regarded this area as constituting a very important distinction because the short simple sentence 'does not facilitate the communication of ideas and relationships which require precise formulation', but only permits logical modification and stress at a fairly low level. In addition, according to Bernstein, the public language tends to emphasize *'things'* rather than *'processes'*. (Perhaps this is a more acceptable formulation of the content/structure point I criticized in Paper I.) In referring to characteristic 6 of the public language, 'sympathetic circularity' (later termed socio-centric sequences), Bernstein considered this a very important category because such sequences, when used repeatedly, discourage further analysis, and close the discussion at that particular level: 'Curiosity is limited in such a way as to enhance the solidarity of the social relationship.' Characteristic 7. In this kind of utterance, although the medium is verbal, the message is frequently non-verbal i.e. social: the real meaning being conveyed is, 'do as you're told because . . .' Similarly categories 8 and 9 also are used in order to reinforce social solidarity rather than communicate unique messages. Characteristic 10 indicates that, whereas the formal language expresses meaning which is logically explicit and finely differentiated, with a public language meaning is implicit and crudely differentiated.

In concluding this paper, Bernstein suggested that the implications of a public language were (a) logical (b) social and (c) psychological. The psychological implications included not only the orienting and cognitive aspects already mentioned, but also the fact that many lower working-class patients would be unable to benefit from psycho-therapy because of the form of the social relation and the mode of its communication (see also Bernstein, 1964, not dealt with here).

Comment

(1) This paper clarifies two of the three issues commented on in connection with Paper I. (a) It clarifies Bernstein's attitude to the Whorfian hypothesis that 'language is one of the most important intervening variables between the individual and behaviour' and 'it would seem that linguistic form orients the individual in one direction rather than another and once this direction is given it is progressivly reinforced'. (b) The content/structure distinction is abandoned, never to reappear, and is replaced by a much clearer statement: 'The linguistic form is a powerful conditioner of what is learnt, how it is learnt and so influences future learning.'

(2) Some difficulties in the description of public and formal language remain: (a) the ten characteristics of public language and the eight characteristics of formal language comprise an unsystematized mixture of items, some of which are objective and easily measurable, others which are vaguely defined and extremely difficult to measure objectively; (b) in public language, characteristic 1 'poor *syntactic construction*' is not defined and might be taken to mean non-standard, incorrect grammar rather than illogical, incomplete or ambiguous structures; (c) characteristics 9 and 10 are not clearly defined nor exemplified.

(3) Whilst there was some attempt to connect public language with social structure, there seemed to be little indication that use of public or formal language might vary with region, ethnic group, religion etc. (This possibility has in fact never yet been explored.)

I have made a number of criticisms of this paper but it should be noted that it was intended by Bernstein as an exploratory paper—a first attempt to make rather more explicit the 'embryonic' suggestions of the first paper, rather than a complete systematization of his theory.

Paper 3. 'Social Structure, Language and Learning' (1961)

In this paper, intended to be read by teachers, Bernstein suggests that the problem for the lower working-class (public language using) pupil becomes acute at the secondary level of education when the discrepancy between what he can do and what he is called upon to do, widens. The reason for this is that during the secondary stage the educational curriculum becomes more and more analytical and relies on what Piaget classified as formal operations, whereas the lower working-class pupils are more likely to be restricted to concrete operations.

In explaining why lower working-class children develop in a way which is educationally limiting, Bernstein develops and makes more explicit his theory of the relationship between social structure and language, 'there is little doubt that the social form of a relationship acts selectively on the mode of and content of communication'. He quotes Vygotsky in support of the idea that the closer the social relationship, the less the need to make meaning fully explicit, 'communication goes forward against a backcloth of closely shared identifications and affective empathy which removes the need for elaborate verbal expression' and in this kind of relationship the content of the communication is likely to be concrete and descriptive rather than analytic and abstract. Bernstein suggests that, because lower working-class children grow up hearing and using *only* this kind of language in a social structure which does not facilitate any other kind of communication, they will inevitably be at a disadvantage in learning situations where less limited forms of language are necessary.

In this paper Bernstein also develops his notion of differences in the experience of guilt. Bernstein suggests that an important *correlate** of a public language is that the individual will feel *shame* (i.e. responsibility to the group) rather than guilt (which involves the internalization of values). He refers to the work of Kohn (1959) to show that middle-class parents tend to respond in terms of the child's *intent*, whereas working-class parents respond in terms of the immediate consequence of the act itself. Thus there is little verbal investigation of motive and discipline.

Although not fully developed in this paper it is interesting to note the genesis of the ideas on the authority relationship between mother and child which is to feature as the social control typology in Bernstein's later work. It is also important to

* I think Bernstein was particularly careful to use the word 'correlate' and avoid 'consequence'.

note that implied in this paper is the importance of the discontinuity between home and school in terms of the forms of social control employed by the mother on the one hand and by teachers on the other; this again is a point developed in later papers.

Comment

(1) The exact relationship of social structure, language and learning is still not clear in this paper. It is not made explicit where 'cognitive mode' fits in to the general model. Does its omission from the title of this paper suggest its theoretical redundancy? This point will be discussed in the general discussion of models at the end of this chapter.

(2) It is perhaps surprising that Bernstein makes no mention of the numerous studies of deaf children in his discussion of language.

Paper 4. 'Social Class and Linguistic Development: A Theory of Social Learning (1961)

In this paper Bernstein's theory is introduced by means of a survey of previous studies of language, environment and intelligence. This is very useful since it enables the reader to set Bernstein's work in some kind of historical context. It is in this paper that Bernstein uses the phrase 'linguistic determinism':

it is proposed that two distinct forms of language use arise because the organization of these two strata is such that different emphasis is placed on language potential. Once the emphasis or stress is placed then the resulting forms of speech progressively orient the speakers to distinct types of relationships of objects and persons. The role intelligence plays is to enable the speaker to exploit more successfully the possibilities symbolized by the socially conditioned linguistic forms. There are exceptions to this *linguistic determinism,* which arise under special limiting physiological and psychological conditions. It is suggested that the typical and dominant mode of speech of the middle-class is one where speech becomes an object of special perceptual activity and one where a theoretical attitude is developed toward the structural possibilities of sentence organization. This speech mode is one where the structure and syntax are relatively difficult to predict for any one individual and where the formal possibilities of sentence organization are used to clarify meaning and make it explicit. This mode of speech will be called a formal language.

Comment

(1) It is a little difficult to know exactly what is meant by 'a theoretical attitude is developed toward the structural possibilities of sentence organization'. Presumably Bernstein means that middle-class children are more aware that there is a linguistic rule system which can be manipulated according to context, but this is not entirely clear in the passage.

(2) The introduction of the notion of predictability as a defining characteristic of the two codes may be a useful factor in enabling these two language forms to be objectively distinguished but to say that in the public language 'speech elements are *highly* predictable for any one speaker' is slightly misleading. In accordance with this definition of the theory it would only be necessary to state that public language sequences are more predictable than formal language. The whole question of predictability as the defining criteria will be discussed later in this chapter.

II. EXPERIMENTAL WORK

This work was of course contemporaneous with the early theoretical papers but for the sake of clarity of presentation has been considered separately to see to what extent the experimental data supports the original hypothesis.

Experimental Paper 1—Language and Social Class (Research note 1960)

This paper is a first report of a study designed (1) to extend and confirm the 1958 Paper which suggested that the two speech modes were related to different status groups and (2) to show that the orientation of the two linguistic forms was independent of non-verbal intelligence test scores.

Prediction. Bernstein predicted that in the working-class group the language scores would be severely depressed in relation to the scores in the higher ranges of non-verbal intelligence tests. The sample consisted of sixty-one boys aged fifteen to eighteen of working-class background (they were messenger boys, none of whom had been to grammar school) and forty-five boys of the same age from a public school. The tests used were Raven's Progressive Matrices and the Mill Hill Vocabulary scale.

Results.

(1) *Mean raw scores—Non-verbal.* Working-class 47·4, public school 51·4 (i.e. the public school sample had an average score three points higher than the working-class); *Verbal.* Working-class 41·9, public school 60·2 (i.e. public school were on average 18 points superior). If these scores were translated into I.Q. equivalents it would mean that the public school boys were 8–10 I.Q. points superior on the non-verbal test but 23–24 I.Q. points superior on the verbal tests.
(2) The verbal scores of the working-class group were depressed in relation to scores at the higher ranges of the non-verbal test. This relation was not found in the public school group.
(3) Almost all of the working-class group had scores confined to the average range of the verbal test.

Bernstein drew the following conclusions from this experimental work: (1) that a different relation existed between verbal and non-verbal I.Q. for the two social groups; (2) that a score of a verbal test was a powerful indication of educational performance as well as 'ability'; (3) that either the mode of expression of intelligence was a cultural factor or that the lower working-class were *genetically* deficient in a factor which enabled the exploitation of complex verbal relationships. Considering the relatively deprived linguistic environment of the working-class group, the former alternative was more likely.

Comment

This was a small sample but it is important to note that the discrepancy in verbal and non-verbal I.Q. has since been found in a number of other studies, including Venables (1959) reported in the Crowther Report, Ravenette (1963) and an unpublished study of the Institute of Education, University of London.

Experimental Paper 2—Linguistic codes, Hesitation Phenomena and Intelligence (1962)

The aim of the experiment had already been stated in connection with Experimental Paper 1, namely, (1) to see whether the two codes were associated with social class, (2) to see whether the orientation to one or the other was independent of I.Q. The method used was a tape-recorded, relatively undirected discussion on capital punishment. Measures of verbal planning were taken according to the Goldman Eisler technique of hesitation phenomena (i.e. measuring frequency and length of pauses in speech sequences). The sample consisted of five groups each containing five boys. Groups 1 and 2 were middle-class boys, groups 3, 4 and 5 were working-class boys and the groups were selected to enable the following comparisons to be made: (1) a general inter-class comparison; (2) class comparisons with non-verbal intelligence held constant; (3) class comparisons with verbal and non-verbal intelligence held constant; (4) comparisons between different I.Q. profiles holding class constant. Bernstein made the following predictions associated with elaborated and restricted codes: (1) Holding verbal and non-verbal I.Q. constant, working-class groups would pause less frequently and spend less time pausing than middle-class groups. (2) Holding non-verbal I.Q. constant, working-class groups would pause less frequently and spend less time pausing than middle-class groups. (3) Irrespective of non-verbal I.Q. the hesitation phenomena of working-class subjects would be similar. (4) A general relationship would be found between the two I.Q. tests for the working-class group. The verbal scores would be severely depressed in relation to the scores at the higher ranges of the non-verbal test. It was expected that this general relationship would not hold for the middle-class group. (This final section of the experiment has been reported in Experimental Paper 1.) The speech sample consisted for each group of the eighteen hundred words which followed the first five minutes of the dis-discussion. In accordance with the experimental work of Gold-man-Eisler, utterances were divided into long and short utter-ances (short utterances were considered to be those containing less than forty syllables). The two categories of utterances were analysed separately.

Results. (1) Overall social class differences were found. As pre-dicted, working-class subjects used a longer mean phrase length, spent less time pausing and used a shorter word length. (2) Holding non-verbal intelligence constant, social class differ-ences were found in the same direction. (3) Holding verbal and non-verbal intelligence constant, social class differences were again found in the same direction but not for word length. (4) Within the middle-class group the sub-group with superior verbal intelligence used a longer mean phrase length, a faster rate of articulation and a longer word length. (5) Within the working-class group the sub-group with the average I.Q. profile spent less time pausing.

Conclusions. Goldman-Eisler (1954) had demonstrated that sum-marizing, abstract speech was associated with longer pauses and more frequent pauses. Bernstein demonstrated that hesitation phenomena were associated with social class differences in speech behaviour. The conclusion reached was that these speech differences were evidence of two linguistic codes elabor-ated and restricted, which entailed qualitatively different verbal planning orientations which controlled different modes of self-regulation and levels of cognitive behaviour.

In addition to describing this experimental work, the paper also set out the theory very clearly. (1) the rather misleading terminology public and formal language were replaced by restricted and 'elaborated' codes. (2) there is a clarification of the theoretical model. 'The social structure transforms language possibilities into a specific code which elicits, generalizes and reinforces those relationships necessary for its continuance.' (3) a wider area of sociological investigation is indicated: 'One of the tasks of the sociologist would be to seek the social origin of particular linguistic forms and to examine their regulative function.' (4) in addition to this kind of clarification of the theory, it is also developed in as much as restricted code is sub-divided into pure restricted code (lexical prediction) and restricted code (structural prediction). (5) the sociological conditions for these two codes are carefully specified. (6) it is made clear that the code exists only in terms of verbal planning operations. (7) the association of elaborated and restricted codes with social class is made clear. 'An elaborated code is associated in middle-class and adjacent social strata. These codes, however, are not necessarily clear functions of social class, but in advanced industrialized societies the association will have a high degree of probability. Class is only one of many principles of social stratification and differentiation.'

Comment

Although the theory is undoubtedly clarified in this Paper, two main difficulties remain: (1) the definition of the codes in terms of predictability without their being tested by this criterion; (2) the sub-classification of restricted code into lexical prediction and structural prediction. These two points will be discussed later in this chapter.

It is very surprising and perhaps unfortunate that this paper has received less attention than the earlier formulations of the theory. It is unfortunate not only that even recent publications still quote Bernstein's work using the less precise terminology 'public and formal', but also that the real importance of this imaginative and original experiment is sometimes overlooked. Other sociological and social psychological studies (quoted in Chapters I and II) had suggested a relationship between social background and such character traits as impulsiveness: the importance of Bernstein's experiment was that it demonstrated for the first time an objective difference in behaviour: in other words Bernstein devised a method of measuring a process which had hitherto merely been inferred. This experiment is also important inasmuch as it showed that restricted code and elaborated code are not simply different 'styles' of speaking on a par with dialect differences but are related to different kinds dimension of verbal planning, the conclusion being that restricted code users were habituated to 'short run' searches in their verbal planning operations. If this assertion is true, and it is very much in line with impressionistic studies of working-class intolerance of ambiguity and delay (see Klein, 1965), then it has very far reaching educational implications.

Experimental study 3—Social Class, Linguistic Codes and Grammatical element (1962)

Using the same samples of working-class and middle-class boys' language, as in the previous study, Bernstein proceeded to analyse the material using methods of conventional grammar.

Results. (1) No social class differences were found in the proportions used of finite verbs, nouns, prepositions, conjunctions and adverbs.

(2) 'I think' (referred to as egocentric sequence) was found to be much more frequently used by middle-class boys, whereas the sympathetic circularity sequences (e.g. 'wouldn't it', 'isn't it', etc. referred to as 'socio-centric' sequences) occurred more frequently in working-class speech.

(3) The middle-class groups used a higher proportion of: (a) subordinate clauses; (b) complex verbal stems; (c) passive verbs, (d) total adjectives and uncommon adjectives; (e) uncommon adverbs and conjunctions; (f) 'of' as a proportion of 'of', 'in' and 'into'; (g) personal pronoun I.

(4) The working-class groups used a higher proportion of (a) total personal pronouns; (b) 'you' and 'they'.

Comment

(1) In this paper, as in the previous experimental paper on hesitation phenomena, the codes were defined in terms of predictability. 'The structural elements are highly predictable in

the case of a restricted code and much less so in the case of an elaborated code.' The differences in frequency between one social class and another on the various linguistic measures, although statistically significant, are not so great as to justify using the term '*highly* predictable'.

(2) Not all the recognition criteria of restricted and elaborated codes (listed in the 1959 paper) have been tested for social class differences. This may be because not all of them are testable in this way (see general comment below).

(3) The value of this paper lay especially in that the previous findings relating to hesitation phenomena, verbal planning and abstract, concrete levels of language were now related to linguistic forms. For example ego-centric and socio-centric sequences were tied to certain roles and role relations and therefore another *objective* indication of code was made available. Similarly Bernstein's exploratory socio-linguistic treatment of pronouns is important.

(4) Bernstein's criteria for form classes (for example 'uncommon' adjectives and adverbs etc.) are too arbitrary to be satisfactory.

(5) No measure of Bernstein's own contribution to the discussions was included and no indication of the continuity of the discussion or the frequency of interruptions. (See Chapter VI for suggested experimental improvements in these last two cases.)

III. LATER THEORETICAL PAPERS

'A Socio-Linguistic Approach to Social Learning' (*1965*)

Since this is the most recent paper it might be expected that it would be the clearest exposition of overall theory. It presents no new evidence but relates Bernstein's thesis to a wider framework—a socio-linguistic framework, which is explained historically as well as conceptually.

In this context Bernstein sets out clearly his own intellectual stance towards the so-called Whorfian hypothesis, and objects to the notion of 'fashions of speaking' which are neither related to an institutional order nor emerge from structure of social relationships, but determine social relations via the general culture. Bernstein, on the contrary, sees social structure as the determining factor in this complex of inter-relations, that is, for Bernstein social structure generates linguistic forms which in turn 'transmit the culture and so constrain behaviour'.

The two codes, restricted and elaborated, are defined once again in terms of predictability and sub-classified in the following way: *Restricted Code* (1) Restricted code lexical prediction (the pure form of restricted code); (2) Restricted code syntactic prediction (narrow range of lexis; inclusive social relationship); and *Elaborated Code* (low syntactic prediction); (1) elaborated code inter-personal relations (2) elaborated code object relations.

Comment

(1) The latest development of the theory by sub-dividing elaborated code into 'object and personal' is a very interesting feature but as it is presented in this paper is rather ambiguous. 'It is possible to distinguish two modes of an elaborated code. . . .' This is ambiguous as it might possibly be interpreted either as a theoretical possibility or as an aspect of the theory which had been tested empirically. The former is in fact the case but this is not absolutely clear in the text. This development is of very great potential importance since it relates the E.C. 'person' and E.C. 'object' to role-learning.

(2) Culture, context, code and role seem to have become basic terms in the new system, and these terms create greater flexibility in the use of the thesis and thus gives it greater generality—it is not simply a matter of social class and language, but of wider questions of culture and linguistic behaviour. Bernstein's linguistic transformation of role, code and socialization is now explicit (despite the fact that a new range of problems now arise relating to problems of code switching etc.).

General Comments

With the publication of this latest theoretical paper 'A Socio-linguistic Approach to Social Learning' (1965) the theory, despite its great complexity, has been expressed in a very lucid way. A number of difficulties remain, however, which have been referred to in the discussion of individual papers above.

Defining the two codes in terms of predictability is not without its attraction but it has also certain difficulties. For example, a Shakespearian speech which was sufficiently well-known to the audience, a ritualistic prayer and a cocktail party conversation are by this method of classification grouped together in accordance with the predictability hypothesis, but if these texts were analysed linguistically, they would be very different. To test the restricted code empirically, using the predictability method, would involve ascertaining not what was said, but how frequently it had been said before. For example, from the point of view of verbal planning, a guide's description of the Vatican, for example, would be in a restricted code because it would be 'well organised', but in terms of any grammatical analysis it would certainly be classified as elaborated code.* This example simply illustrates the difficulty of defining the codes in terms of predictability but testing them in terms of grammatical analysis or hesitation. In fact, the test of predictability has never been applied to working-class and middle-class speech samples, and the empirical difficulties involved would be enormous.

The meaning of 'Predictability'

It is not clear exactly what is meant by the term predictability in Bernstein's writing. Does it mean a percentage score for class elements or syntactic combinations ? In this case would it be better to talk of relative frequencies? (Clearly they are related.)

It would seem that Bernstein had not, at the time of writing, examined a sufficient number of texts to give an exact linguistic description of a restricted code. Probably for this reason he used general terms like predictability. If the term predictability is

* Bernstein has stated (private communication) that in his terms a spoken text might consist of very elaborate speech but if it were highly predictable—as with the Vatican Guide—it would be restricted code because it would be used as ritualized aspects of a set of positional relations: it is the role relation rather than the linguistic structures which are the primary determiners of code, although usually this is reflected in the linguistic structures of the speech.

used in any sense it is also necessary to ask where predictability is possible, at what choice-points does it occur?

The Meaning of 'Restricted' and 'Elaborated'

Bernstein's Papers (1962, a and b) which provide the objectively measurable link between code and verbal planning, would seem to imply that at the linguistic level it ought to be possible to establish basic linguistic units which distinguish elaborated and restricted codes. In a restricted code the basic unit will tend to be a longer 'string' than in elaborated code: it will be a well-organized combination. In elaborated code on the other hand the basic unit will be shorter—i.e. in an utterance of a given length more choice-points will occur. Moreover in the elaborated code at every choice-point in the syntactic system there is a greater element of discretion, for the syntactic combinations created at such choice-points. A wider range of options is available. Thus in the elaborated code there will be flexibility at the syntactic level whereas in restricted code there will be rigidity in the nature of choices. In order to determine the location of such choice-points it will be necessary not only for more texts to be examined but more texts from a wide variety of contexts.

The above is some attempt to make more precise, although it is still rather vague, the definition of restricted at the linguistic level. However, Bernstein's work also indicates other dimensions to the concept restricted:

1. It refers to a restriction of the range of social contexts from which issue appropriate linguistic performance. (Role Restriction.)

2. Restriction also refers to the range and types of referents which are verbally transformed and elaborated. This would seem to have cognitive, affective and evaluative consequences, and thus affect learning. (Referential Restriction.)

3. Restriction also appears to refer to the range of individuals who share the code. (Restriction in Scale.)

A number of questions remain. First the empirical question—is it the case that restriction at the linguistic level is followed by restriction in the other three behavioural dimensions? Second, is it the case that an individual limited to a restricted code is different from an individual possessing elaborated code because he possesses a much more limited knowledge of the linguistic rule system? Bernstein's choice of words in the 1961 Paper 'A theoretical attitude is developed toward the structural possibilities of sentence organization' would seem to indicate his opinion that the working class have a nascent awareness of the rule system but that their social structure and culture does not lead them to explore it and *develop* it nor to innovate within it to the same extent as elaborated code users.

The elaborated code is the exact converse of the above, with the further distinction of object and person relations. It therefore becomes necessary to obtain linguistic measures of object and person relations as well as an explicit definition of the role-learning which these two modes of an elaborated code presuppose.

The progression of the thesis in the papers can be seen in the progressive elaboration of the basic model: in the first paper the model seemed to be a simple one, as portrayed in Figure 1:

Social structure →language →mode of cognitive →educational
                                expression   attainment

In the later papers this model appeared to have become more complex.

Figure 2

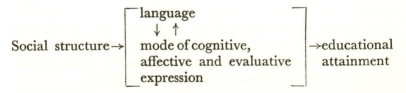

However, the latest paper actually specifies a much more complicated model.

Figure 3

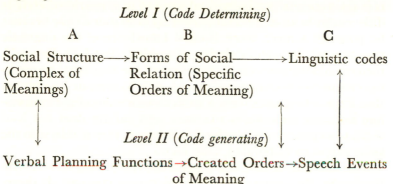

Level I (Code Determining)

A | B | C

Social Structure⟶Forms of Social⟶Linguistic codes
(Complex of Relation (Specific
Meanings) Orders of Meaning)

Level II (Code generating)

Verbal Planning Functions→Created Orders→Speech Events
of Meaning

'The arrows indicate reciprocal influence as it is possible for a verbal planning function to develop which creates novel orders of meaning and social relation.'

It may be that the latest model has a great deal more to offer, but this has not been explained in the text of the paper and indeed is of such complexity that it perhaps deserves a paper in itself to offer a complete explanation of this theoretical model. However, this is perhaps simply the difference between looking at a model which formulates the present theory rather than one which is formulating wider implications of the theory as yet untested. The difference between Level I and Level II is a difference in level of abstraction. Level I is the sociological level, Level II is its psychological or social psychological correlate. It therefore represents Bernstein's thesis as an attempt at methodological individualism, i.e. that any sociological argument or thesis must be driven down to the level of the individual actor. In this respect the model attempts to make explicit what Firth said about social context (see Chapter IV). Bernstein is essentially concerned with socialization and the transmission of culture; therefore codes are seen as transformations of the critical roles in the socialization process. On this basis the four critical roles are: (1) The kinship role. (2) Age group roles. (3) Educational roles. (4) Work roles. It would therefore be theoretically possible to find linguistic evidence for four basic codes relating to the four critical roles; empirical work in this field has yet to be attempted. The model behind Bernstein's restricted code is Durkheim's concept of mechanical solidarity. The model behind the elaborated code is that of Durkheim's 'organic solidarity'. Mechanical solidarity here refers to how people relate to each other through similarity of function in a society; and organic solidarity refers to the kind of social structure whose members relate through dissimilarity of function. If this is the case then the origin of Bernstein's thinking lies not in any linguistic tradition but in Durkheimian sociology.

The importance of the existing theory is that it relates social structure, verbal planning, language and educability. It was for this reason that Bernstein's hypothesis was chosen as a way of looking at the problem of social class, language and learning. Despite some of the minor reservations about detail of the presentation of the theory, mentioned above, it still represented the most profitable way of looking at the problem of social class and educational performance and in particular the linguistic differences between social class groups. It was for this reason that the experimental study, to be described in detail in Chapter VI, was designed in that form. The Bernstein theory was obviously very interesting and of potentially great applicability but, at the time this study was initiated, the evidence did not seem to be conclusive. It seemed, therefore, that an appropriate course of study would be (1) to duplicate Bernstein's group discussions on capital punishment but also to look at slightly younger children as well as those at the end of their secondary school career. (2) To test the existence of linguistic differences in terms of restricted code and elaborated code in a speech situation other than a group discussion (i.e. individual interview) and to vary the level of coding difficulty. (3) To discover to what extent these speech differences would carry over into the written language. Details for these three sections of the experimental work of this study will be given in Chapter VI.

VI

AN EXPERIMENTAL STUDY OF THE SPEECH AND WRITING OF SOME MIDDLE- AND WORKING-CLASS BOYS

This chapter contains a brief account of my own research work on the speech and writing of four small groups of secondary school boys in the London area. The reasons for undertaking this work were firstly to duplicate Bernstein's research on social class language differences in group discussion situations, i.e. to produce confirmatory evidence of the theory or to refute it; secondly to extend the range of evidence by collecting 'discussion' speech from some boys younger than the subjects used by Bernstein; and thirdly to investigate other kinds of speech situations and the written language of the same boys.

Owing to the large amount of work entailed in linguistic analysis of this kind, it was decided to limit the sample to four groups of five boys and to concentrate on detail and a variety of contexts rather than produce a superficial analysis of a large number of subjects. A more complete account of this work has been given elsewhere (Lawton, 1963, 1964, 1965).

The twenty boys were selected from two schools. The first school was a London secondary modern school in a working-class area; the second was an independent fee-paying school in a middle-class suburb of London. All four groups were matched for verbal and non-verbal intelligence on the Mill Hill Vocabulary Scale and Raven's Progressive Matrices. All the boys selected were of average verbal and non-verbal intelligence.

The social class of the working-class groups was checked by an examination of the school Record Cards, using the occupation of the father as the determining criterion; for the purpose of this study working-class was regarded as synonymous with manual worker. The social class of the middle-class groups was checked by explaining the criterion used (i.e. those whose fathers were in social class I or II of the Registrar General's Classification) to the Headmaster who was able to confirm that all the boys selected were unquestionably middle-class.

It should perhaps be stressed that the working-class boys selected for this experiment were certainly not the most linguistically 'backward' that could be found. The school from which they were drawn has a very high reputation compared with the other secondary modern schools in the district; the pupils come from 'respectable' rather than 'rough' working-class families; four out of the five working-class fifteen-year-old boys remained at school for a full year after the compulsory leaving age. On the other hand the independent school mentioned in the experiment was not the most expensive in the district; in common with many schools of this type it was not without its staffing problems, and it appeared that the turn-over of staff there was at least as great as that of the secondary modern school; also classes were only very slightly smaller (25–26 pupils) than at the secondary modern school. It should be noted, therefore, that the social difference between the middle-class and working-class groups was much less extreme than the distance between the groups in Bernstein's study.

I. WRITTEN WORK: ESSAYS AND SENTENCE COMPLETION TESTS

I visited each group of boys in a classroom in their own school, and on six successive weeks asked them to write four 30-minute essays and two Sentence Completion Tests. The essay subjects were as follows:*

1. A story ('Urashima the Fisherboy') was read to the group and they were immediately asked to re-write it.
2. 'Home'.
3. 'My Life in Ten Years' Time'.

* The essay titles used are slightly modified forms of the essays suggested by Schonell (1942).

4. A foreigner who has heard of 'soccer' but never seen it played wants to get to know and understand the game. Explain to him carefully how soccer is played.

The two Sentence Completion Tests used were Watts' Multiple Choice Sentence Completion Test, and an open-ended Sentence Completion Test which I constructed myself to test the pupils' ability to create sentences of different lengths and complexity.

For compositions 2 and 3 no guidance was given and no discussion invited or permitted on what kind of essay was expected. The title was simply written on the blackboard and the boys were told, as they were for titles 1 and 4, that they would have thirty minutes to write and that they would be told five minutes before their time was up.

Results

(See Lawton (1963) for further details and statistical tests used etc.)

Length of Essay. The most obvious difference between the groups was that at each age level the middle-class boys wrote significantly longer essays in the half-hour period. At age twelve the average length of essay for the working-class boys was 210 words compared with the middle-class average of 289; at age fifteen the average length was working-class 228, middle-class 348. The fact that boys of very similar measured ability produce such strikingly different amounts of written work in a 30-minute period needs close examination. I am sure that by any criterion the working-class essays would not be rated more highly than the middle-class; therefore it cannot be argued that the working-class groups produce quality rather than quantity: this possibility is supported neither by the other linguistic measures used in the analysis nor by impressionistic examinations of the content. In fact the reverse trend seems to be true: that to maintain the quality of work even at this standard the working-class boys in some cases reduce their quantity, especially when writing on the more 'abstract' subjects of 'Home' and 'My Life in Ten Years

Time'. It should also be stressed that there was no noticeable difference between the groups in 'finishing early': in all groups there was a degree of pen-sucking and staring at the ceiling but it was not apparent that the working-class boys gave up or finished very much before time.

The most likely explanation of these differences in output is that for a Restricted Code user expression of ideas in writing, especially in the formal medium of an essay, is much more like an act of translation than is the written expression of middle-class boys. It is probable that the verbal planning required for writing is much closer to the verbal planning of the Elaborated Code than the simpler verbal planning processes associated with Restricted Code. No detailed analysis of this can be attempted here but it did appear that those occasions when working-class boys wrote fairly long essays their written style was much closer to speech, whereas the shortest working-class essays were unsuccessful attempts at abstract impersonal writing. The following is the complete result of thirty minutes' writing by a working-class twelve-year-old boy making some attempt at abstract writing:

Home

Home is a place where you are looked-after. parents run it so you are ordered to do things. you are comfetable and your mum does the house work you do homework

House home mean the same But in different ways you might be posh and you might be poor if you live in a slum it's nothing to be ashamed. Some slums are al right some houses are worse than slums as long as you have a roof over your head you are all right you can buy a notice what says 'HOME SWEET HOME' They have agent what find out where other people Blacks will turn England into india They take up our homes.

The general impression gained from an examination of the working-class essays is that the working-class pupils found writing a difficult exercise, and found writing on abstract topics very difficult indeed. This is very much in accordance with Vygotsky's view:

Written speech is a separate linguistic function, differing from oral speech in both structure and mode of functioning. Even its minimal development requires a high level of abstraction. It is speech in thought and image only, lacking the musical, expressive, intonational qualities of oral speech. In learning to write the child must disengage himself from the sensory aspects of speech and replace words by images of words. Speech that is merely imagined and that requires symbolization of the sound image in written signs (i.e. a second degree of symbolization) naturally must be as much harder than oral speech for the child as algebra is harder than arithmetic. Our studies show that it is the abstract quality of written language that is the main stumbling block, not the under-development of small muscles or any other mechanical obstacles.

Unfortunately we do not know the precise nature of Vygotsky's investigations—it is very important therefore that more studies should be carried out in this field.

Subordination. One of the conclusions of many of the studies reviewed in Chapter III was that the degree of 'subordination' used in written work frequently distinguished middle-class from working-class writers (as well as being a general indication of 'maturity'). In this study an index of subordination was obtained for each essay by dividing the total number of subordinate clauses by the total finite verbs. This measure yields slight but not statistically significant differences between the working-class and middle-class boys. However, the impression gained from reading through the essays was that the working-class boys tended to use a relatively narrow range of types of subordinate clause, and were achieving a fairly high 'subordination' score mainly by means of adverb clauses of 'time' and noun clauses used as 'objects' of the main clause. Other studies have also shown that 'object' clauses are very common and are learned very early in life, whereas noun clauses used as 'subject', 'complements' and 'in apposition' are much later language sophistications. In this study they are fairly uncommon in the middle-class writing (twenty-nine examples) but almost non-existent in the working-class groups (four examples). The same applies to adverb clauses, some of which are used very frequently by quite young children (e.g. time) whereas the clauses of result, concession, etc. are much later developments. In this study therefore a count was made excluding these two classes of subordinate clause (i.e. noun clause object and time clauses) and this measure was referred to as 'uncommon clauses'. This measure then showed significant differences between the contrasted groups: the group mean score for the working-class twelve-year-olds was 0·13, middle-class twelve-year-olds 0·18; working-class fifteen-year-olds 0·17, middle-class fifteen-year-olds 0·19. However, the more recent studies quoted in Chapter III agreed that 'maturity' of expression is marked not only by an increase in the frequency of use of subordinate clauses, but also in the complexity of their structuring. Several attempts have been made to measure this kind of complexity, and I decided to employ Loban's Weighted Index of Subordination, which has the merit of taking some non-finite constructions into account as well as finite. Loban's method is to divide all subordinate clauses into four categories:

A. A subordinate clause which is directly dependent upon a main clause. (First order dependence) = 1 point.
B. A dependent clause modifying or placed within another dependent clause. (Second order dependence) = 2 points.
C. A dependent clause containing a verbal construction (i.e. infinitive, gerund, participle) = 2 points.
D. A dependent clause modifying or placed within another dependent clause which, in turn, is within or modifying another dependent clause. (Third order dependence) = 3 points.
The 'Loban Score' was thus obtained and divided by the total number of words written to compensate for the greater length of middle-class essays. The results obtained show clearly that the ability to use subordinations of greater complexity than the first order dependence may be an index of age development but that class differences are more important. One disadvantage of the Loban Score is, however, that an individual can score highly simply by using a sufficiently large number of A-clauses—even if it were the same clause pattern each time. To overcome this disadvantage a ratio was taken of B, C and D clauses to total

subordinate clauses. These figures then tended to show greater social class differences than the simple Loban Score. (The working-class twelve-year-old boys produced 19 B, C or D clauses compared with the middle-class twelve-year-olds 54, the working-class fifteen-year-old boys 41, and the middle-class fifteen-year-olds 89.)

Passive Verbs. Although the total number used by any group was fairly low, the social class difference is one of the most remarkable. The total number of passives used by each group is as follows: working-class twelve-year-olds 23, middle-class twelve-year-olds 56, working-class fifteen-year-olds 35, middle-class fifteen-year-olds 86. To compensate for the tendency for the middle-class boys to write longer essays, the total passive verbs written by each boy was divided by total finite verbs. The mean figure for each group then became working-class twelve-year-olds 0·04, middle-class twelve-year-olds 0·07, working-class fifteen-year-olds 0·06, middle-class fifteen-year-olds 0·1. This is a statistically significant difference for the twelve-year-old group but not for the fifteen-year-olds, although the trend is clear. The passive verb structure is an obvious example of an impersonal form which is more suitable for less concrete kinds of writing.

Personal Pronouns. A number of the studies referred to in Chapter III regarded a diminishing percentage of pronouns as an indication of increasing maturity of writing. The results obtained in this study show social class to be even more important than age as a factor. When total personal pronouns are divided by total words the following indices are obtained: working-class twelve-year-olds 0·074, middle-class twelve-year-olds 0·054, working-class fifteen-year-olds 0·055, middle-class fifteen-year-olds 0·049. These differences are statistically significant at both age levels. Two interpretations are possible to explain this social class difference: it may be that the working-class boys are insufficiently specific, using pronouns where a noun or noun phrase would be more appropriate, or this may be a carry-over from speech where the use of a pronoun combined with a non-verbal signal can adequately communicate in many concrete situations, but, as Symonds and Daringer (1930) showed, when the writing takes on a more impersonal and abstract nature the percentage of pronouns falls.

Adjectives and Adverbs. Two counts were made of adjectives: the first was of the total number of adjectives used in the four essays, and this showed differences, but not significant differences, between the social class groups because the working-class boys tended to use the same adjectives over and over again. The second count was of 'uncommon adjectives'. This measure was obtained by excluding all repetitions of an adjective and all those which occurred in the list of the 100 most commonly used words (McNally and Murray, 1962). This measure showed a clear tendency for the middle-class boys to use a wider variety of adjectives.

The same kind of pattern of social class differences was observed for adverbs. Middle-class boys used not only more adverbs but also a wider variety.

Vocabulary. A count was made of the total number of words used in the four essays which are contained in the list of 'most common 100 words'. These totals were then expressed as a percentage of the total words used. The group mean figures are as follows: working-class twelve-year-olds 61 per cent, middle-class twelve-year-olds 56 per cent, working-class fifteen-year-olds 57 per cent, middle-class fifteen-year-olds 55 per cent.

This measure was used with the expectation that although the vocabulary of comprehension of the matched groups of the same age could be assumed to be very similar (because they were matched on the Mill Hill Vocabulary Scale), the words they actually selected for *use* would be different: i.e. the working-class boys would select from a narrower range of alternatives. It is of course not a very delicate measure but it does indicate that two slightly different selection processes are operating. It has been suggested that the social class differences shown above as crude percentages are likely to be under-estimates of the real difference between the groups because the average length of the middle-class essays is greater. The same argument applies here as was used by Estoup (1917) in a discussion of the 'Type Token Ratio', i.e. that as the length of a passage is increased it becomes more likely that words will be repeated, and less likely that new words will be used.

This measure supports the findings regarding adjectives and adverbs and shows the working-class groups to be over-employing common words. This is important because it shows clearly, as was suggested by Vygotsky (1962), that although extension of vocabulary is an important factor in development, knowledge of a word's meaning does not ensure its use in speech or writing.

Content Analysis: Abstraction and Generalization. Bernstein's thesis maintains that there is a relation between speech systems and the orientation towards abstract formulation. I made the prediction that this would be reflected in written work provided that there was sufficient choice in the handling of the essay subject. For two of the four titles ('Home' and 'My Life in Ten Years' Time') it was possible to write personally or impersonally, abstractly or concretely. The boy had the choice, for example, of describing his own home or writing about home in a more generalized way. Similarly, although the title of the third essay was given as 'My Life in Ten Years' Time' he could still write about it from the point of view of how he would be different in ten years' time, or how the world would be different and how that difference would affect his life. To measure this difference as objectively as possible the essays were scored on the following four point scales by four examiners working independently of each other, and whose level of agreement with each other turned out to be remarkably high (co-efficient of concordance was 0·78 for 'My Life in Ten Years' Time' and 0·89 for 'Home').

Abstraction Scale: 'Home' and 'My Life in Ten Years' Time'.
(A) Completely abstract.
(B) More than 50 per cent abstract.
(C) More than 50 per cent concrete.
(D) Completely concrete.
Generalization Scale: 'Home'.
Does the writer mention his own home . . .
(A) Not at all.
(B) For less than 50 per cent of the writing.

(C) For more than 50 per cent of the writing.
(D) All the time.
Generalization Scale: 'My Life in Ten Years' Time'.
Does the writer mention his own life . . .
(A) Not at all.
(B) For less than 50 per cent of the writing.
(C) For more than 50 per cent of the writing.
(D) All the time.

The two scales (abstraction and generalization) are usually closely connected but not always: for example it is possible for a boy to write about his own home all the time without being completely concrete if he mentions 'love' or 'security' etc.

Scoring system:
(A) counts as 3 points.
(B) counts as 2 points.
(C) counts as 1 point.
(D) counts as 0 points.

The total of the four judges' scores were as follows: working-class twelve-year-olds 56, middle-class twelve-year-olds 111, working-class fifteen-year-olds 86, middle-class fifteen-year-olds 139.

An analysis of this kind does not, of course, show that the working-class boys were incapable of writing with a high degree of abstraction: all that this experiment showed was what in fact they chose to do, but the content of the essays certainly reinforces the view that the working-class world is dominated by concrete things rather than by ideas, by events rather than reflections on those events.

Working-class fifteen-year-old boy's essay on

My Life in Ten Years' Time

I hope to be a carpenter just about married and like to live in a modern house and do a ton on the Sidcup by-pass with a motor-bike and also drinking in the Local pub.

My hobby will be breeding dogs and spare time running a pet shop. And I will be wearing the latest styles of clothes.

I hope my in ten years time will be a happy life without a worry and I have a good blance behide me. I am going to have a gay and happy life. I am going to work hard to get somewhere in the world.

One thing I will not do in my life is to bring disgrace and unhappiness to my family.

Middle-class fifteen-year-old boy's essay on

My Life in Ten Years' Time

As I look around me and see the wonders of modern science and all the fantastic new developments I feel a slight feeling of despondency. This is because I am beginning to wonder who will be in control of the world in ten years time, the machine or man. Already men are being shot round earth in rockets and already machines are being built that will travel faster and faster than the one before. I wonder if the world will be a gigantic nut-house by the time I'm ten years older. We are told we will be driving supersonic cars at fantastic speeds, with televisions, beds, and even automatic driving controls. Do we want this, do we want to be ruled by machinery. Gone will be the time when the family go out for a picnic on a Sunday Afternoon, we will be whisked along wide flat autoroads, we will press a button in a wall and out will come a plate of sandwiches ready prepared. you may think that this is a bit far-fetched but if things keep on improving men will not have to think for themselves and we will become a race of bos-eyed mawrons. There is, if this is going to happen, no way to stop it. Men say we will have just one or two more luxuries and it never stops. I enjoy the luxuries of to-day, but in my opinion there is a limit. But who decides what that limit will be. No one knows its just a lot of men all relaying on someone to stop this happening, but no-one is going to. We're doomed. No prayers can save us now, we'll become slaves to great walking monstrosities. Powerless in the hands of something we helped to create. I'm worried about 'my life in ten years time'.

It is also worth noting that it was on the two essays 'Home' and 'My Life in Ten Years' Time' that the greatest differences in length emerged between the working-class fifteen-year-old boys and the middle-class fifteen-year-old boys. Whereas for the story reproduction and the essay on soccer the middle-class group wrote about 30 per cent more, with the two more abstract essays the middle-class boys wrote an average of nearly twice as much. If the reasonable assumption is made that the quantity of the written result is related to the difficulty of the task, it seems likely that when faced with an opportunity of writing in an abstract way the working-class boys either try, but find it difficult and write very little, or they try, find it difficult and then revert to concrete description. There are several essays which support this view: for example, the working-class fifteen-year-old boy who wrote the two most abstract essays, wrote very little—'Home' 118 words, 'My Life in Ten Years' Time' 149 words—far below the average even for his group. Another boy wrote 123 words in fairly abstract terms, but then stopped in the middle of a sentence and concluded the essay with a completely concrete description of his house. . . .

Home

Home can be from a dustbin to a castle. Some people has to make do with sleeping on a park bench, also people make do with a hostel as home such as the Salvation Army Hostel for men. The best home is of course is the house which you and your family run when you can come home when you like and find your bed waiting for you and have meals ready on the table for you. The people who have lodgings are sometimes have a land lady telling you off all the time about noise if you have your own home you are your own boss. It is much cheape if you lived in your own house than a boarding house because

My home is a house about 120 years old at the back of the House is a stable. the garden is a fair size We have six rooms. In front of our house there is a double pavement.

(Working-class 15-year-old boy)

Sentence Completion Tests

The two tests were chosen to contrast 'passive' or 'receptive' understanding, and 'active' or 'expressive' construction. The Watts Multiple Choice Sentence Completion Test involves no more than the ability to select the sentence ending which makes sense and to reject the three that do not make sense. For example, item 1 of the Watts Test is

(1) I shall not be able to do my sums UNLESS . . . .
(a) they are too difficult; (b) you help me; (c) multiplication is very hard; (d) they are marked by you.

The pupil is required to underline the group of words which would make the best sense.

The Watts Test was therefore simply a means of testing the comprehension of various connectives, and since the boys had been matched for their performance on a vocabulary scale no social class differences were predicted. On the other hand the open-ended test was constructed especially for this experiment to test not the ability to recognize structures but to formulate them into sentence patterns, and in this task I predicted that as the sentences became longer the social class differences would become greater: the middle-class boys would choose to select subordinating constructions whereas the working-class boys would use compound sentences, or their constructions would break down completely and force them to start a new sentence.

Sentence Completion Test

Complete the following sentences using the number of words in brackets. You may finish the sentence in any way you please as long as it makes sense, but do not make it into two or more sentences.

Example:

    A. The man said he was going............(add one word).
       The man said he was going home.
    B. The admiral went...........................(add ten words).
       The admiral went to China six times when he was in the navy.

Now complete the following:

1. I am sorry...(add 4, 5 or 6 words).
2. The teacher said.....................................(add 8 to 10 words).
3. The boy asked...(add 12 to 14 words).
4. If I were you I..(add 14 to 16 words).
5. The Prime Minister made.....................(add 16 to 18 words).
6. When I was...(add 18 to 20 words).
7. We went for a walk...............................(add 20 to 22 words).
8. I could not join them............................(add 22 to 24 words).
9. The boy's answer was...........................(add 24 to 26 words).
10. My house is near the place...................(add 26 to 28 words).

The first four sentences were regarded as an easy 'warming-up' exercise, and only sentences 5 to 10 were scored and analysed. There was no time limit.

One indication of the processes at work in this test can be gained simply by comparing the relative frequencies of co-ordinations and subordinations (i.e. mainly the use of 'and', 'so', and 'but', compared with other conjunctions). A more refined measure is to divide the total subordinations for each individual by the total finite verbs used by that individual. These results are shown in the Table below.

TABLE 4

Open-Ended Sentence Completion Test

	Total Co-ordinations	Total Sub-ordinations	Total Subordinate Clauses (finite and non-finite): Total finite verbs
Group 1 (WC 12)	33	31	0·26
Group 2 (MC 12)	11	42	0·44
Group 3 (WC 15)	19	28	0·33
Group 4 (MC 15)	19	42	0·48

The importance of this test is that it shows that when length is eliminated as a variable the working-class boys still use fewer subordinations, preferring to select a series of short units or several short units strung loosely together by 'and', 'so' or 'but'.

Although it is important not to exaggerate the value of these results since the numbers involved are very small, they do provide some evidence that the characteristics of Bernstein's Restricted Code carry over into the writing of working-class boys of secondary school age. The consistency of the results indicates that social class differences exist not only in vocabulary, but also in whole classes of words (adjectives, adverbs, pronouns), and in structures (passive verb forms and types of subordination). In each case working-class boys select words and structures from a narrower range of alternatives. Moreover the abstraction and generalization tests indicate that the kind of linguistic differences described above are in fact associated with differences in the *content* of the written compositions. I think that this is probably the most important aspect of this part of the study.

II. SOCIAL CLASS LANGUAGE DIFFERENCES IN GROUP DISCUSSIONS

The purpose of this second part of the study was to provide data comparable with that contained in Bernstein's Paper (1962 b), secondly to compare the results of fifteen-year-old boys with those aged twelve, and thirdly to make possible a comparison of the written and spoken modes of language of the same boys.

Each of the four groups was asked to discuss the question of capital punishment, the topic used by Bernstein (1962). In each case I introduced the subject for discussion myself and kept the direction of the course down to minimum. Each discussion lasted approximately thirty minutes, but the number of words spoken by each group was not exactly the same, partly because some discussions lasted a few minutes longer, and partly because in some cases more pauses occurred and it was necessary for me to give more probes in order to keep the discussion going.

In each case the whole length of the discussion was used for the analysis, but to make comparison possible with Bernstein's results (1962) the same exclusions were made for the purposes of analysis: i.e. fragments, repetitions, socio-centric sequences, together with 'I mean' and 'I think' were omitted from the analysis.

Results (See Lawton (1964) for further details, statistics etc.)

'Ego-centric' and 'Socio-centric' Sequences. Bernstein's study showed that the working-class boys used more socio-centric sequences (e.g. 'You know', 'Isn't it?', etc.) whereas the middle-class boys used the ego-centric sequence 'I think . . .'. The following Table shows that similar results were found in this study at both age levels.

TABLE 5

Ego-centric: Socio-centric Sequences

Group	Total Ego-centric (I think)	Total Socio-centric (Isn't it, etc.)	Ego-centric: Socio-centric
WC 12	34	40	0·8
MC 12	46	24	1·9
WC 15	20	65	0·3
MC 15	46	23	2·0

Subordinate Clauses. As with the samples of written work described above, differences between the social groups were found at each age level on the simple index of subordination, but social class differences were more striking when they were examined for depth or degree of subordination by means of the Loban Score. Trend differences in the predicted direction were obtained for adjective clauses and uncommon clauses but were not statistically significant.

In Bernstein's study of group discussions he had used a measure which he termed *complexity of verbal stem.* Bernstein's criterion of complexity was three or more words in the verbal stem, or a verb plus an infinitive. 'Complex' verb stems were counted and divided by the total number of finite verbs. The prediction was that middle-class groups would use more complex verbs than the working-class groups. This prediction was confirmed in this part of the study, with the additional result that social class differences at age fifteen were greater than at age twelve. (But see below for a possible qualification of this result.)

Passive Verbs. In the study of written work reported above the frequency of passive verbs was found to be a most important method of distinguishing the middle-class and working-class groups. Similar results were found in the speech used in this discussion situation, indicating that social class differences are much greater than the intra-class age differences. Since this is an interesting and consistent social class difference, some theoretical explanation would seem to be called for. Unfortunately very little detailed work has been produced on the passive voice: Chomsky (1957) treats the passive as a single transformation from the active voice, but the work of Harwood (1959) would suggest the necessity of making sub-divisions within what has traditionally been called passive, and the extreme rarity of passive forms in children's language might suggest that more complex processes than one transformation are involved. Jespersen's (1924) comments on the use of passive, although very limited in scope, are of some relevance to the present study. He suggested five possible types of use:

1. Where the active subject is unknown or cannot easily be stated.
2. Where the active subject is self-evident from the context.
3. Where there are special reasons like tact or delicacy for not mentioning the active subject.
4. Where the passive is preferred even if the active subject is indicated because interest is focused on the passive subject (the 'converted subject') rather than on the active subject. e.g. 'The house was struck by lightning.'
5. Where the passive may facilitate connection between one sentence and the next: e.g. 'He rose to speak and was listened to with enthusiasm.'

There are of course uses of the passive which would seem to be unnecessarily complicated and undesirable, but all five of Jespersen's categories are examples of fairly sophisticated usage requiring a high degree of control over the language forms; although it might be argued that in theory anything could be expressed in English without ever using the passive voice, in practice its absence or low frequency is probably symptomatic of a limited control over language use.

Personal Pronouns. A significant difference was found between the working-class boys and the middle-class boys at age fifteen but not at age twelve (i.e. the working-class boys used a higher percentage of personal pronouns). It would seem that the frequency of use of personal pronouns, far from being a trivial habit, may be a good indicator of control over 'impersonal' language—a form which would have been the most appropriate for the discussion in this part of the study.

Adjectives and Adverbs. Significant differences were found between the two groups of fifteen-year-old boys (middle-class using more adjectives and adverbs and also selecting from a wider variety), but not between the twelve-year-old boys. This negative result for the two twelve-year-old groups, however, needs some qualification. It seems most likely that the middle-class group's low scores on a number of measures in this discussion situation was due to the kind of discussion that took place. Unlike the other three groups which kept to calm exchanges of opinion this discussion on capital punishment rapidly developed into a very heated argument, and as Goldman-Eisler (1961) has demonstrated the frequent interruptions in this kind of situation will tend to lower the intellectual quality and the level of verbal planning:

> Discussions are a type of situation which allows for a mixed bag of operations. Automatic verbalization of well-learned sequences will alternate with the utterance of words and expressions individually selected and fitted to the occasion, with the new formulation of general statements, etc. The proportion of each type of speech, and the level of speech planning will depend on the type of discussion, the demands made on the speaker either by interlocutor, or theme, or other factors in the situation, the speaker's individual disposition, or the time factor inherent in the situation and the extent to which it is inimical to delay.

Unfortunately, it was not possible to analyse the hesitation phenomena (i.e. the pausing) of these discussions, since the background noise in the school was too great to enable accurate analyses to be made by means of the equipment used by Goldman-Eisler and Bernstein. Thus Goldman-Eisler's measure of phrase length could not be used to test the suggestion that the middle-class twelve-year-old group's discussion was measurably different from the others; however, the quality of the discussion can be examined objectively simply by counting the number of interruptions that occurred in each discussion. In the middle-class twelve-year-old discussion group there were 121 interruptions, a very much higher figure than any one of the other three (working-class 12, 4 interruptions; working-class 15, 19; middle-class 15, 0). A count was also made of the number of times that I made any contribution or probe: for the middle-class twelve-year-old discussion group I gave far fewer leads or probes than any other group (working-class 12, 66 leads, probes etc.; middle-class 12, 16; working-class 15, 65; middle-class 15, 40). Thus there are two factors operating which should be taken into consideration when the two twelve-year-old discussion groups are compared: on the one hand the working-class group was receiving more support, questions and guidance from me which would tend to raise the level of discussion; on the other hand the nature of the middle-class twelve-year-old discussion was likely to lower the level. If the groups were in other respects equal it would be expected that the group with many interruptions and little support from the interviewer would make lower scores on the kind of measures used in this study; since in fact the scores of these two groups are very similar it would be reasonable to assume that potentially the middle-class group would have a greater degree of language control and would, for example, be able to choose from a wider range of adjectives and adverbs if the discussion had been of a less hectic nature.

Content Analysis of Group Discussions. In Bernstein's study of group discussions the 'content' of each discussion was evaluated by means of an analysis of the hesitation phenomena (see Chapter V above); unfortunately this was not possible with my recordings, but I felt that a useful alternative would be to examine the content of each discussion impressionistically and to attempt some kind of classification. It appeared to be possible to put all intelligible utterances into four categories:

(A) *Abstract* argument (in terms of retribution, deterrence, protection of society etc. although not necessarily using these words).

(B) Hypothetical example explicitly illustrating a *Category* (e.g. 'A man who is drunk when driving and accidentally kills someone, does not deserve to hang because he did not kill intentionally').

(C) Hypothetical case used simply as a *concrete example* (e.g. 'If I'd done a murder I'd expect to get hung').

(D) *Cliché or Anecdote* (e.g. 'An eye for an eye, a tooth for a tooth', 'On the television the other night its this story its called').

My prediction was that all groups would make responses from all four categories but that working-class boys' utterances would be mainly C and D whereas middle-class boys would use a higher proportion of A and B.

TABLE 6

Content Analysis: Percentage of Utterances falling into each of four Categories

Group	A (Abstract)	B (Category)	C (Concrete)	D (Anecdote cliché)	
	%	%	%	%	
WC 12	1	29	51	19	(100)
MC 12	22	33	30	15	(100)
WC 15	1	25	71	3	(100)
MC 15	12	70	15	3	(100)

The social class differences emerge quite clearly from this analysis, but there would appear to be no age differences of importance. Another point which has been commented upon by those who have listened to the tapes or read the transcripts is the tendency for working-class boys to fix upon an example and examine all its possible complexities, relevant and irrelevant, but still fail to make any kind of generalization from it. Similarly another working-class characteristic is that when they are 'given' a hypothetical example to illustrate a whole category (B), they tend to interpret it as a specific, unique, concrete case (C), and proceed to discuss it in these terms: for example, when asked to consider drunken drivers who accidentally cause death the working-class twelve-year-old boys' discussion proceeded as follows:

C.R. 'Well, although, it, it is partly the driver's fault for having too much to drink and he can't control the car the pedestrian should also look out to see if there's any cars coming before he crosses.'

D.L. 'Yes so what would you decide in a case like that?'

C.R. 'Well. He would be guilty of you know having too much to drink, drunken driver but I wouldn't accuse him of, you know, killing anybody.'

D.L. 'Right, yes, B.L.?'

B.L. 'Well sir, I'd take his licence away for a start give him a short time in prison and, um, then . . . er . . . never let him, make him . . . er . . . whatever you do don't let him drink for a long while, keep him in a locked room and put, um, put alcohol in the vases of, um, flowers like I see on the telly once and they get sick of alcohol, they get drunk and they get sick and they don't like it no more and, um, they, they never touch spirits again unless, unless by mistake like I see on the telly, this lady she was an alcohol and she ordered tomato juice and this other lady had a vodka and tomato juice and it looked very like the same but she drunk by mistake the vodka and tomato juice so she phoned her, phoned her wife up, her husband up and he was, he was a doctor. so she says I've, I've by mistake I've drunk vodka so she, so he says, come to hospital straight away and then . . . er . . . I'll give you an injection to make you better you know so she, so she was just on her way out so she went over to the bar and she says "Vodka and tomato juice" and she kept drinking that and then she got alcohol again but if they keep doing that then you should put them in life imprisonment for the murder what they'd done previously.'

This example also illustrates the tendency to 'drift' from C to D (anecdote). An even more striking example of this kind of reversion to the concrete came later in the same discussion:

D.L. 'Well, what do you think should make us decide whether to hang a man or not then? What sort of rules should we try to draw up about whether a man ought to be hanged or not?

B.L. 'That, that man, I don't know his name, I know it was Joseph, he had, I think, had killed a lot of people about eight and he had another four lined up he was going to murder. It was in the papers his name was Joseph something. Well he should have been hanged 'cause nothing would have stopped him really I don't think, after he had done one murder. Some people, they murder people then they-s-get frightened and they never do it again unless they're really forced to but that man done it eight times already he murdered people and I think they should have hung him to stop him hurting other people and it'd be better for him really.

Naturally the middle-class groups also use anecdotal material, but in general there tends to be a move away from the concrete example to a generalization even if the link is not completely clear:

G.I.   'Look at Eichmann, he killed six million Jews and one look at him he's got a conscience.'

S.Y.   'Yes.'

G.I.   'He must have a guilty conscience.'

S.Y.   'Yes well he's not the sort of person who cares but I expect after these people who've murdered somebody they're in a state of madness and they don't know what they're doing you know.'

(Middle-class 12-year-old group)

What is not shown by the above table of results is the degree of difficulty experienced on those occasions when the working-class discussion focused on abstract formulation:

'Bit of advantage hanging them, isn't it? It's a bit . . . sort of person who's lost their well say a person's husband's what's murdered well he's after about 20 years and he's free again well he'll, might start again. You'd want to see him hanged, wouldn't you and out of the way.'

(Working-class 15-year-old)

This was clearly an attempt to argue for capital punishment in order to protect society but the difficulty involved in coding this was very great.

Certainly the overall impression gained from this kind of examination of the discussions is that the working-class boys, where they have a choice, tend to move towards concrete situations and real or imaginary specific examples; when they attempt to discuss in abstract terms they find difficulty in doing so.

TABLE 7
Comparison with Bernstein's Results

Group Mean Score:	This Study WC 12	MC 12	WC 15	MC 15	Bernstein (1962) WC 16	MC 16
1. Subordinate clauses: finite verbs	0·39	0·41	0·33	0·45	0·34	0·50
2. Complexity of verbal stem	0·10	0·13	0·10	0·18	0·12	0·17
3. Total adjectives	0·07	0·06	0·08	0·09	0·05	0·08
4. Uncommon adjectives	0·03	0·02	0·04	0·05	0·02	0·04
5. Uncommon adverbs	0·02	0·02	0·02	0·03	0·02	0·04
6. Passive verbs	0·06	0·07	0·05	0·12	0·04	0·09
7. 'Of': 'Of', 'in', 'into'	0·26	0·20	0·45	0·36	0·54	0·60
8. All personal pronouns: words	0·13	0·13	0·12	0·09	0·08	0·07
9. I: personal pronouns (total)	0·15	0·20	0·24	0·25	0·16	0·37
10. I: words (total)	0·02	0·03	0·03	0·03	0·02	0·03
11. You and they: personal pronouns (total)	0·34	0·48	0·48	0·37	0·44	0·33
12. You and they: words (total)	0·04	0·06	0·06	0·03	0·04	0·03
13. Selected personal pronouns: words	0·12	0·12	0·09	0·07	0·09	0·07
14. I: personal pronouns (selected)	0·08	0·12	0·14	0·22	0·16	0·25
15. I: words (selected)	0·01	0·01	0·02	0·02	0·01	0·02
16. You and they: personal pronouns (selected)	0·34	0·54	0·49	0·40	0·43	0·32
17. You and they: words (selected)	0·04	0·06	0·05	0·03	0·04	0·02
18. Words excluded from analysis	16·6%	18·1%	15·0%	8·6%	9·7%	7·2%

The table above compares the group mean scores of my four groups with the results of Bernstein's sixteen-year-old middle-class and working-class boys of average I.Q. The list of results includes all the measures which are common to the two studies, and also those measures used by Bernstein but which have not been discussed in detail in this study.

The interesting feature of this comparison is that in most

cases the results are very close, and in all cases except one the social class difference between groups is in the same direction. This may be regarded as a confirmation that, even if the measures used are crude, they seem to show differences which are most unlikely to arise by chance; secondly it would seem that Bernstein, using a much smaller number of words for each subject, obtained results very similar to those in the present study. An interesting exception to the agreement of results is the percentage of words excluded from the analysis. The words excluded were 'I mean', 'I think', socio-centric sequences, words repeated and fragments. The last two items were defined as 'False starts and sequences which could be deleted without altering the meaning'. It may be that the difference between the two studies in this percentage was caused by the subjective element in deciding what can and cannot be deleted without altering the meaning. This is a minor criticism of the method employed. It may also indicate that methods of analysis which have been used for group discussions have paid insufficient attention to the function of these 'false starts' and repetitions. It would seem that they may serve the purpose of preventing others from talking while the speaker organizes his own future utterances—a willingness to say anything rather than risk an interruption. This is, however, speculation based on general impressions of the four discussions rather than a systematic attempt at a detailed examination of these items.

The data provided by this part of the study must undoubtedly be regarded as confirming the evidence presented by Bernstein's work on group discussions. A number of differences were demonstrated between the social groups at both age levels, and, as with the written work, differences were greater at age fifteen than at age twelve (with the qualification noted above). The measured social class differences were, however, generally slightly less than those found in the study of written language.

III. SOCIAL CLASS DIFFERENCES IN INDIVIDUAL INTERVIEWS

The purpose of this final part of the study was to test the Bernstein hypothesis regarding Elaborated and Restricted Codes in a critical situation where it would be possible to control the level of coding difficulty, and to contrast the performance of the groups differing in age and social class in two kinds of speech situations labelled 'Description' and 'Abstraction' (Goldman-Eisler, 1961).

Each boy was interviewed individually by the writer in a quiet room provided by the school and the whole of the interview was tape-recorded. I had already met the middle-class boys on two previous occasions for the I.Q. testing and group discussions, so that the subjects were not faced by a complete stranger; the working-class boys knew me since I had spent several months in the school and had taught some of them for a few weeks. The interview started with some easy routine questions asking the boys their full name and age etc., the purpose of which was to allow the subjects time to settle down comfortably to the interview situation. The interview itself was divided into three sections:

1. Four sets of picture cards: each set consisted of four or five cards which conveyed a story. The subjects were first asked to describe the pictures (description), and then to abstract the point of the story (abstraction).
2. Questions about school involving first descriptive, then abstract language.
3. Four questions involving moral judgements (abstraction).

The structure of the interview was kept the same for all twenty boys (see the full interview schedule later in this Chapter).

The interviews lasted approximately twenty minutes each. The number of words spoken by the subjects, excluding the introductory sequences, ranged from 406 words to 1,683 words with a mean of 950. No attempt was made to limit any contribution: the subjects were allowed to continue until they clearly had no more to say.

The whole of the language used in the interview was analysed (except the short introductory sequence), and to make comparison possible both with Bernstein's results and with the speech of these same boys in group discussions, the same exclusions were made as for the second part of this study reported above. Finally, the speech sample for each boy was divided into two

categories of 'description' and 'abstraction' according to the
position of the sequence in the structure of the interview: the
sequences following the instructions to describe the pictures, to
describe their school and to describe the teachers they remembered clearly were classified as 'description', whereas the
sequences following the request to give the point of the pictures,
those following the questions about the purpose of education
and the qualities of good teachers, as well as the answers to the
four final moral questions were all classified as 'abstraction' and
were analysed separately.

INTERVIEW QUESTIONNAIRE

Question	*Purpose of question*
1. Will you tell me your full name, please?	
2. And your age?	To obtain factual information, and
3. And your date of birth?	to allow the subject to settle down.
4. Good. Now, have you always lived in ....?	
5. I am going to show you a series of pictures which form a complete story when put together. I want you to describe each picture one by one: This is the first picture......... Now this one......... And the next .... And here is the last picture	To test subject's ability to use descriptive and abstract speech.
6. Now look at the pictures all to-gether and tell me what you think the point of the story is If no response to 6:	
6a. Summarize the story as briefly as as you can. Now give the story a suitable title. (Repeat procedure for 5 and 6 for each set of pictures.)	
7. How long have you been at this school?	To provide a natural link with 9.
8. What school did you go to before you came here?	
9. Now, I should be very interested to know how much you remember about your previous school. Tell me about it.	To obtain a fairly long sample of natural descriptive speech.

10. Now you have already spent a lot of your time and energy at school. What do you think is the real purpose of education?

    If no response to 10:

    To raise the speech to an abstract level.

10a. All this school and education—what's it all for?

11. Let's go back to your previous school again—tell me about the teachers you can remember most clearly. . . .

    Descriptive speech and introduction to 12.

12. What qualities would you expect a really good teacher to possess?

    If no response to 12:

    To test the ability to answer an abstract question in abstract terms.

12a. You must have come across good and not-so-good teachers? What is it about some teachers that makes them better than others?

13. Now, I'm going to ask you some questions about things that we often take for granted—but it is sometimes interesting to ask why. You don't have to answer in one sentence—there are no points—not a question of right or wrong but your opinion:

    To test the ability to verbalize on abstract moral questions.

    (i) In a shipwreck, why should women and children be saved first?

    (ii) Why should a promise be kept?

    (iii) Why are criminals locked up?

    (iv) Do you think it is a good idea for films to be classified U, A or X?

Results (See Lawton (1965) for further details of results, statistics, etc.)

The Number of Words Spoken in the Interview. The total number of words spoken by the subjects ranged from 406 to over four times that number, but no pattern emerged which would justify thinking that the quantity of speech elicited was connected either with social class or with age.

The Number of Words Excluded from the Linguistic Analysis. This is a convenient means of measuring the total number of fragments, repetitions and unfinished utterances. In seventeen out of the twenty cases the percentage of words omitted from the 'abstraction' sequences is greater than the percentage of fragments, etc., in the 'description' sequences. This would seem to indicate that the percentage of false starts, fragments and repetitions occurring in a passage may well be an indication of coding difficulty and level of verbal planning. A second difference of some interest is that at both age levels there are differences between the social class groups in the percentage of words excluded: although in neither case are the differences statistically significant, it is worth noting that at each age level the middle-class boys have a slightly higher percentage of fragments etc. than the corresponding working-class group. A further difference, worthy perhaps of further study, is the fact that the percentage of words omitted decreases with age in both social classes.

Summary of Other Linguistic Results

Social Class Differences at age twelve. (a) On the sections of the interview designated '*description*': there were no significant differences, but there were trends* on four measures (adjective clauses, Loban B, C and D clauses, adjectives, passive verbs). (b) On the sections of the interview designated '*abstraction*': there were significant differences on three measures (ego-centric/socio-centric sequences, passive verbs, personal pronouns); there were also trends in the predicted direction for a further four measures (adjective clauses, uncommon clauses, Loban B, C and D clauses, adjectives).

Social Class Differences at age fifteen. (a) '*Description*' sections: significant differences were found on three measures (Loban B, C and D clauses, adjectives, passive verbs); there were also trends on another two (adjective clauses, uncommon adverbs). (b) '*Abstraction*' sections: significant differences were found on

---

* Differences were regarded as trends when there was at least 25 per cent difference between group means and/or when the u-test was only one or two places beyond a significant level.

three measures (ego-centric to socio-centric sequences, passive verbs, personal pronouns); there were also trends in the predicted direction on a further five counts (adjective clauses, Loban B, C and D clauses, complex verb stems, total adjectives, uncommon adjectives).

Code-Switching. One of the basic assumptions of Bernstein's theory (1958) was that Elaborated Code speakers would tend to be able to switch from one code to another according to the demands of the situation whereas the Restricted Code user would tend to be confined to one code. Nine out of the thirteen measures used in this study were regarded as possible indicators of code switching: the four measures excluded were adjectives and uncommon adjectives, adverbs and uncommon adverbs. The reason for the exclusion of these four counts on the code switching comparison was that although a high proportion of adjectives and adverbs have been regarded as one of the criteria for Elaborated Code usage, it could still be predicted that in a summarizing/abstracting task a reduced number of adjectives and adverbs would be elicited when subjects give succinct responses (Goldman-Eisler, 1961). Thus, although the abstract sequences would demand Elaborated Code, there will also be the tendency to reduce 'unnecessary' elaborations. It was therefore predicted that of the nine remaining measures all four groups would make some linguistic adjustments to the difference in context between the 'description' and the 'abstraction' sequences, but that the middle-class groups would make greater adjustments than the working-class groups: i.e. the middle-class boys would possess greater facility in code switching.

The first part of the prediction was confirmed by the fact that on all measures except those relating to adjectives and adverbs a majority of boys scored more highly on abstraction than on the description sequences. (Note: code switching was measured by the difference between a score on abstraction and the score on description, referred to later as the A-D score. See Table below). The second part of the prediction, i.e. that the middle-class boys would 'code switch' *more* than the working-class boys, was shown by the fact that the middle-class twelve-year-old boys reached a higher average degree of code switching on all nine measures, and the fifteen-year-old middle-class boys made greater adjustments on seven measures. (The working-class fifteen-year-olds' A-D score was higher on subordinate clauses; on the Loban Score the middle-class and working-class A-D score was identical.)

TABLE 8

Discussion: Linguistic Measures
Group mean scores

		WC 12	MC 12	WC 15	MC 15
1. Ego-centric:	(description)	1·0	0·4	0·13	0·0
socio-centric	(abstraction)	0·56	18·0	0·46	15·0
2. Sub clauses:	(description)	0·197	0·136	0·206	0·201
finite verbs	(abstraction)	0·322	0·394	0·519	0·454
3. Sub adj. clauses:	(description)	0·020	0·033	0·031	0·054
finite verbs	(abstraction)	0·024	0·048	0·023	0·066
4. Uncommon clauses:	(description)	0·097	0·085	0·105	0·109
finite verbs	(abstraction)	0·186	0·242	0·234	0·257
5. Loban score:	(description)	0·032	0·031	0·026	0·028
words	(abstraction)	0·066	0·087	0·093	0·094
6. BCD clauses:	(description)	0·139	0·189	0·040	0·070
total sub clauses	(abstraction)	0·185	0·324	0·280	0·349
7. Complex verb stems:	(description)	0·108	0·057	0·088	0·094
finite verbs	(abstraction)	0·148	0·143	0·132	0·215
8. Total adjectives:	(description)	0·081	0·096	0·089	0·093
words	(abstraction)	0·064	0·074	0·054	0·068
9. Uncommon adjs:	(description)	0·032	0·035	0·030	0·037
words	(abstraction)	0·024	0·031	0·024	0·031
10. Total adverbs:	(description)	0·082	0·094	0·088	0·091
words	(abstraction)	0·082	0·078	0·083	0·080
11. Uncommon adverbs:	(description)	0·018	0·021	0·021	0·028
words	(abstraction)	0·026	0·025	0·017	0·020
12. Passive verbs:	(description)	0·023	0·044	0·018	0·065
finite verbs	(abstraction)	0·012	0·087	0·038	0·123
13. Personal pronouns:	(description)	0·120	0·110	0·089	0·079
words	(abstraction)	0·121	0·096	0·100	0·077

Content Analysis

Apart from the introductory, 'settling down' questions at the beginning of the interview and the linking questions, there were three sections to the interview: (1) picture story cards, 'description' followed by 'abstraction'; (2) questions about schools and teachers, 'description' and 'abstraction'; (3) questions on moral subjects which called for only abstract answers. It was predicted that there would be no social class differences on the description passages, but that to some extent the middle-class responses to the abstraction sequences should reflect their greater power of code-switching and greater control over language. The results of the contest analysis were as follows:

1. *Picture story cards* (Question 6). No social class differences were detected.

2. *Teachers and schools* (Questions 10 and 12). The responses to question 10 could be classified into two main categories: those given by boys who thought that the purpose of education was vocational, and those who thought it was a general preparation for 'life'—some boys, of course, gave both types of response. The 'preparation for life' response was considered to be more abstract. Of the twelve-year-old boys, *all* ten gave the vocational response; in addition, three of the middle-class boys gave the more general reason, but no working-class boys gave this kind of answer. At age fifteen, four working-class and two middle-class boys gave 'vocational' responses; three working-class and all the middle-class boys gave 'preparation for life' responses. Since the number of pupils involved was so small I would not want to claim more than the possibility that this is suggestive evidence of class differences, and worthy of study separately on a much larger scale.

The responses to question 12 tended to be more complex. There were four possible categories of response, and many boys gave more than one 'quality' that they expected good teachers to possess. The four possible kinds of qualities were: 1. that a teacher should possess adequate *knowledge*; 2. certain *personality* characteristics, such as kindness, patience etc.; 3. teaching *skill*; 4. *discipline* or control (often referred to as 'strictness').

No social class difference in the general pattern of results was found either in the kind of response made or in the range. The only noticeable difference was that of 'coding' difficulty—i.e. middle-class boys appeared to find it easier to make the switch to this kind of abstract statement. For example:

B.S. Working-class twelve-year-old

Question 9.* 'Er it was was all right but um I I went on later than this school it didn't end till half past four the infants infants class and the juniors class the infants went out at 4 o'clock so that no-one would get hurt if they both went out together and the juniors went out half past four and er instead of having science they had nature study and things like they had arithmetic and English and they didn't didn't have much geography they had a little bit of history um er we didn't have speech and er well er for games we didn't go out like we do at this school to Beckenham we went round round er well it was a court it was called Tabard Park and we used to play football round there and cricket sometimes.'

Question 10. 'So er the purpose of education is when you grow up suppose you get a better a better job than you would if you didn't learn. And you get more money and it helps you in more ways than one.'

Question 11. 'There was a teacher called um Mr. A. . . . er the headmaster Mr. B. . . . there was a teacher called Miss W. . . . and a teacher called Miss O. . . . Well like Mr. E. . . . he was the teacher in the top class before I left and come to here, I liked him 'cause he was always t-t-tell us interesting things and he's been to lots of places Egypt he's been all over the world. He's travelled a lot and he knew all about all these things and he told us and he was always interesting. And Miss H. . . . did-didn't have her for I wasn't never in her class but I can remember her she was she used to make you do lots of hard work and er there's this teacher called Miss W. . . . and I wasn't in her class but they had easy things they always used to have a lot of games and got easier exams and there was also this teacher called Miss P. . . . she was she just came she just come when I was leaving but and I didn't know much about her. Er.'

Question 12. 'They should you should be well she should be know what she's talking about and she should shouldn't ask something that she doesn't know er to tell us to do something that she would she couldn't do or something like that and er she sh-she shouldn't shout at you every time at you if you've just done something wrong she should warn you I suppose and er she should be worried about bout you your working instead of like some teachers they

* In all cases the interviewer's standard questions have been omitted.

say Oh I'm not worried if if you do it or not but you come back after school. Well they should be worried and they should make you do it at the time if you're playing around or whatever you're doing.'

G.U. Middle-class twelve-year-old

Question 9. 'Well it was at the top of the hill and it was a Catholic school and the teachers there they're called brothers and they're very nice and they it wasn't sort of a very very efficient school and it wasn't as strict as this is but it didn't have its own playing fields. We had to go up the heath to play games and the headmaster was getting on you know was quite old and the not many pupils in my part the you went on to grammar school if you passed your 11+ and if you weren't a catholic then you didn't go on to the grammar school and there's a they they didn't have well the usual lessons of a school I mean they had lessons but the main ones were maths and English I found because of the 11+ they sort of made you work for that more and you did have art but you didn't have history except for the wireless really or geography and m well you didn't have punishments they had a strap.'

Question 10. Well to teach you things so that when you grow up you you'll be able to have a fairly good job according to your brain and be able to get on in life and if you didn't have schooling then well the world would be a dead loss, people wouldn't know much and it just be an ignorant place.'

Question 11. 'M . . . Brother O. . . . he was very he was in the second form the third really and he was the nicest of them I found. He was my last sort of form master when I came to this school m he he seemed to be the most kindest of them you know he always the strap some of them brought it out at the slightest thing but he kept it away for two terms you know he didn't like bringing it out so he kept it away for two terms, very nice.'

Question 12. Well er not to um rush you too much in your work and to take notice of each child individually and the very brainy ones not sort of look after them most and then the backward ones just let them get on with it and not to be late for school for teaching because that sets a bad example unless they've got very good reasons. To be nice to pupils and not to be sort of have a personal grudge against any one of them.'

H.A. Working-class fifteen-year-old

Question 9. 'Oh I remember that there was like three classes and you know there wasn't higher grades but as you got older you went into the next class and so on. Remember there was all women teachers there. There was headmistress er used being mixed with girls like but used to be older girls like up above you. They stayed on at the school the girls while the boys had to go to another one cause it was only girls school the top part of it and er used to be a few nice teachers where er the bit I remember mostly was Mr. P. . . . coming to the school and we had to take the 11 + and waiting for the letter to come to tell me whether I could come here or not or go to some other place. I don't remember much after that.'

Question 10. 'Well I mean you go out and you get a job and they ask you to add up and you say I don't know what these figures mean like you asked a gipsy or anyone like that they don't usually go to school very much. You ask if they can add it up or what's the time they wouldn't know it because they're like stupid they they don't know much, Think the point of going to school is at least you know something when you leave you know. I mean you know what two and two is but you ask the gipsy or anyone like that and they couldn't tell you.'

Question 11. 'In the first class there was Miss P. . . . er yer and I always used to be doing things in her room there and she always used to bang on the desk everything like that . . . didn't like her much. Er second class there was Miss O. . . . and she was all right but you know she didn't used to go off* or give you the cane or that they didn't never used to give you the cane there. The last one was Mrs. C. . . . well she left a couple of years ago but she was the best of the lot before I left like—used to be all right.'

Question 12. 'Well to know to know most of the subjects what they teach at the school.'

B.R. Middle-class fifteen-year-old

Question 9. 'Well if I think I can remember but it doesn't come back to me straight away. I remember the majority of the teachers and the classroom I used to be in. The sort of text books

* 'Go off' is a local idiom for to lose one's temper.

I had. Well its quite a big building um you had to go up some stairs to a landing and there was a a primary school situated at the far end of the playground and the junior school took up the whole of this er double-storey building. Then there was the senior school set apart on another side of the playground.'

Question 10. 'Well, so we'd er make sure that when you're you're into adult life you'll be ready to meet it and you'll be intelligent enough to realise what's going on and be able to look after yourself.'

Question 11. 'Well er we had a very nice maths master as our form master who was very friendly towards us and I got on well with him. He was he taught us a lot of maths and I'm grateful, for, you know.'

Question 12. 'Hm not only the er the facts not only for the teacher to know the facts but to have the ability to put them across to the pupils. Er you have to be very patient to realise that the child is sometimes very slow in learning.'

3. *Abstract moral judgements* (Question 13). The content analysis of this section revealed results very similar to those of questions 10 and 12 reported above—i.e. there were no differences in the level of abstraction reached in answering these 'moral' questions. For example on the third of these questions 'Why are criminals locked up?', the reasons given were classified into four categories (retribution, deterrence, reform, protection of society), but there were no social class differences in preference or range. Once again, however, it seemed to be easier for the middle-class boys to make an appropriate response: the working-class boys often tended to make several attempts before finally hitting the target. Thus for the fifteen-year-old boys, there was no difference in the total number of reasons given by the two groups (each group of five boys gave eight reasons between them), but whereas the middle-class boys needed an average of eighteen words to formulate each reason, the working-class boys needed twenty-four words.

L.E. Working-class fifteen-year-old

Question 13 (i). 'A promise well its er I suppose really it's a matter of honour er if you promise something and you don't keep it er

137

people look down on you as someone who has not dignified . . . In upper classes it's thought to be wrong if you don't keep a promise once er keep er promise a lot of times that people trust you and you'll be able to mm get higher positions. In jobs if you're if you do things efficiently and say that you'll do a certain thing and you don't do it then you wont be trusted so much and someone else can get the opportunities of promotion.'

These results of the Content Analysis, although largely negative in character, are to my mind very illuminating. They confirm the conclusion which I would draw from the linguistic results of this interview speech as compared with the results of the social class differences on written work and group discussions: the inference I would draw would be that in an 'open' situation the working-class boys tend to move towards concrete, narrative/descriptive language, but in a 'structured' situation where they have little or no choice about making an abstract response, they will respond to the demand made upon them. They may have found the task extremely difficult, but it was not impossible for them. From an educational point of view therefore these results justify optimism.

To sum up the results obtained from these interviews I would suggest that because of the critical nature of this situation, i.e. the fact that the boys were in a highly structured context offering a limited range of options, the differences which emerged were smaller than those of the two previous reports on written work and group discussions. Nevertheless, there are social class differences on a number of measures especially those applied to the abstraction sequences. Age differences are clearly less important than social class in this interview situation except in as much as it is important to notice once again that the social class differences at age fifteen are greater than at age twelve.

Perhaps the most important result in this section of the study, however, was the consistent pattern of differences appearing according to whether a sequence was 'description' or 'abstraction'. This is of some importance firstly because it confirms Bernstein's results (1962), and provides suggestive evidence on code-switching; secondly because it indicates the extreme danger of making generalizations about children's language on the basis of only one context (a very common fault in previous research programmes); and thirdly because it indicates that given the existence of Restricted and Elaborated Codes, it would now seem clear that objective linguistic measures of these codes *cannot* be considered as absolutes but will vary according to the situation in which the language is employed. In other words the figures quoted by Bernstein as indices of Restricted or Elaborated Code in his Papers should not be regarded as norms for Elaborated and Restricted Codes, but only as norms for Elaborated and Restricted Codes in a discussion group situation. My results for Restricted and Elaborated Code speech in an interview situation are clearly very different from the results obtained *by the same boys* in a group discussion.

Goldman-Eisler (1961) demonstrated that level of verbal planning was associated with the hesitation phenomena of the speech (i.e. the longer and the more frequent the pauses the higher the level of verbal planning). Bernstein showed that there was a relation also between social class and a tendency to pause longer and more frequently i.e. that working-class speakers tended to be restricted to lower levels of verbal planning. Bernstein also showed that this was associated with linguistic complexity—a low level of verbal planning correlated with a certain lack of grammatical complexity and lack of range of grammatical choices. The present study showed that for *all* groups there was a clear tendency for boys to use more subordinate clauses and more complex constructions in the abstraction than in the description passages. A further point of interest was, however, that although there were differences between the working-class and middle-class boys on the abstraction sequences, these are in fact less great than the differences which appeared in the written tasks or in the discussion situation. There are two possible explanations for this: first, it is clear that the situations used were good for testing the potentiality of a subject to make some kind of linguistic adjustment, but they were probably poor instruments for testing the upper limits of this ability. The highly structured situation at once gave the working-class boys little choice of doing anything but use more complex structures. (E.g. when they were asked 'Why are criminals locked up?' they were forced either to use a subordinate clause or to remain silent. In many cases this question gave rise to a series of subordinate clauses: 'Well because if they were let out they'd be criminals again wouldn't they? I mean they'd go on doing the same thing as what they'd done before, that's why should have the police force. If there wasn't no police force well you'd have all criminals wouldn't you? Wouldn't be no law.' Working-class fifteen-year-old boy—complex speech but lacking a certain coherence.) On the other hand, the middle-class boys were certainly not stretched to the limit of their ability. The interview was not designed to continue making probes at higher and higher levels of abstraction; this would be a very interesting but quite separate study. A second explanation which suggests itself is that in a situation where working class boys are 'pushed', i.e. forced into a situation by a sympathetic interviewer where they have to respond, and are encouraged to go on making responses, they will in fact make some linguistic adjustment. This would suggest that they do have the potentiality available for utterances of an Elaborated Code kind, but they lack practice, and therefore facility. Thus where there is an open choice as in the written essay subjects and sentence completion tests, or in the discussion group situation, they will tend to revert to the kind of language which is most familiar to them and most easy for them to express themselves in. If this is the case then we can be much more optimistic about the possibility of the future education—real education—of such working-class boys. It will clearly be possible, but special techniques will be necessary—perhaps involving more teacher-individual pupil communication. This would provide yet another argument for moving away from the notion of the secondary school teacher's task being the simultaneous instruction of thirty pupils.

GENERAL SUMMARY AND CONCLUSIONS

I. *Written Language*

(a) The first study presented clear evidence that the working-class/middle-class difference in usage of Restricted and Elaborated Code applies to written work as well as speech. This was the first occasion on which Bernstein's theory was tested using essays and other kinds of writing, although the experiment has since been repeated elsewhere and with a much larger number of pupils (e.g. unpublished University of London Institute of Education Papers).

(b) Although there were social class differences even on narrative-description essays, the social class differences were greatest on essay subjects which enabled abstract writing to be selected.

(c) A new Sentence Completion Test was devised which was successful in distinguishing working-class and middle-class pupils in their use of subordinations.

II. *Group Discussion*

(a) In the discussion situation, planned as a replication of the Bernstein experiment, linguistic results remarkably similar to Bernstein's were found, not only in the direction predicted but in the actual numerical scores.

(b) Certain improvements in the experimental technique relating to group discussion have been suggested:

(i) That the contribution of the discussion group 'leader' should be measured by the number of probes, leads and interventions that he found necessary to make.

(ii) That the kind of discussion should be indicated to some extent by counting the number of interruptions which were made by the group members. This is important because a change in the kind of discussion, for example, a heated argument as opposed to a calm exchange of views, is an important change in social context with important linguistic results.

III. *Individual Interviews*

(a) The speech analysis of the individual interviews was of interest for a number of reasons:

(i) Social class differences were still in evidence—i.e. the results were in general in agreement with the prediction according to the Bernstein theory, but

(ii) the actual numerical results were quite different from the figures relating to 'discussion speech'. Thus speech was found to vary not only according to social class, but also according to general context of situation.

(b) Interesting differences were found in relation to description and abstract language, and suggestive evidence on social class differences in code-switching.

(c) As judged by the 'content' of replies to my questions there were very few differences between the middle-class and the working-class boys. In other words, working-class boys' speech did *not* break down completely when they were required to switch to an Elaborated Code as might have been expected, but they obviously experienced coding difficulty.

IV. *General*

(a) These studies show the importance in this kind of work of having several language contexts. In future studies it would be advisable to collect samples of speech and writing from as many different kinds of contexts as possible. Previous studies have tended to assume too much on the basis of a limited number of contexts.

(b) The linguistic measures used have shown some interesting differences, but it is probable that if more delicate measures were used further differences would be made clear.

(c) This kind of linguistic analysis is enormously time-consuming: only small groups of subjects in a limited range of situations could be studied. To do more than pilot work of this kind a team of linguists would be required which could devote its whole time over a number of years to detailed linguistic analysis in longitudinal studies of the same children.

(d) All three studies reported above show greater social class differences at age fifteen than at age twelve. This illustrates the need to study teaching programmes and teaching methods for all age groups: the most rewarding programme would begin with very young children and continue to study their linguistic development over a number of years in relation to their general cognitive development.

(e) The responses of working-class boys to the abstract

sections of the interview suggest that they can be made to use something which is at least approaching an Elaborated Code. They may experience great difficulty, but in this situation, which was intended to be friendly, stimulating and encouraging, their speech did not break down completely. For this reason the experiment may well provide an answer to those critics of 'egalitarian' education, like Bantock (1964), who have used Bernstein's findings as a means of demonstrating the undesirability or futility of trying to educate all sections of the community. Other recent investigations studying cognitive growth have pointed out the extremely large gap between what children conventionally do and what they are capable of doing (Bruner *et al.*, 1966). I would suggest that this study demonstrates a very considerable gap between the normal linguistic performance and the potential attainment of certain working-class pupils.

VII

SOME PROPOSED INTERVENTION PROGRAMMES IN THE U.S.A. AND GREAT BRITAIN

I began this study by looking at a general social-educational problem; it would perhaps be appropriate to conclude the study by examining the practical results of some of the theoretical work which has been discussed. In terms of money spent and the dramatic launching of programmes undoubtedly more is being done in the U.S.A. than in Britain (perhaps because of the more rapid rate of automation and the aggravating problem of race). On the other hand in terms of insightful understanding of the problems the British work may well be further advanced.

PROGRAMMES IN THE U.S.A.

F. Riessman The Culturally Deprived Child (1962)

Riessman's book opens with a startling statement: 'In 1950, approximately one child out of every ten in the fourteen largest cities was "culturally deprived". By 1960 this figure had risen to one in three.' (It is worth noting that no definition of cultural deprivation was given, but nevertheless the problem is clearly an acute one).

Riessman examines the evidence on this problem and concludes that one of the difficulties is certainly the inadequate linguistic ability of large numbers of the 'culturally deprived'. In Riessman's view the Higher Horizons Project in New York City is at least a partial answer to the problem. The Higher Horizons, or Demonstration Guidance Project, was thought to be important not only in its own right but because at the time of Riessman's writing (1962) it had been adopted in thirteen other cities.

144

The Great Cities Improvement Project

The original aim of Higher Horizons was 'to identify, stimulate, and guide into college channels able students from low socio-economic homes'. But the programme was later modified to include all levels of students. The programme, although in detail likely to be unacceptable to British researchers and teachers, is of interest. It includes special remedial classes in reading, together with attempts to improve the motivation of the child and the facilities of the school. At the same time an intensive 'cultural' programme was included to broaden the children's taste in music etc. and meetings were held with parents to gain their co-operation.

Riessman himself was somewhat critical of this programme for two reasons. First he believed the school itself to be insufficiently self-critical, throwing the blame onto the child and his background. Secondly he thought the programme did not go far enough: it still underestimated the potentiality of the 'underprivileged'. In addition to Riessman's criticisms, however, a more serious charge would be that although this kind of programme is useful inasmuch as it demonstrates that such children can be made more amenable to school life, it does not demonstrate how significantly this affects their ultimate intellectual 'improvement'. Moreover the programme is not easily transferable to the whole problem area since it is so costly both in financial and teacher resources. In fact the whole programme has a somewhat guilty, charitable air in its approach—showering good things on the needy rather than carefully analysing the precise nature of the social-educational problem.

Riessman concludes his book by making a number of general comments and recommendations—some of them a little naïve: 1. More teachers should be employed who come from deprived backgrounds themselves. 2. Introspective psychiatric techniques will be less effective for the culturally deprived than physical, authoritative approaches. 3. Progressive education will not appeal to the culturally deprived. 4. School re-zoning should remove segregation. 5. Five or six year college programmes should be organized for slow learners. 6. Schools should be open in the evenings for those with noisy homes. 7. An extended school day and week should be instituted. 8. Smaller classes should be organized, making the best use of teachers skilled in teaching the culturally deprived. 9. Greater use of 'master' or consulting teachers should be made. 10. There should be an increasing use of non-professional personnel in the schools. 11. There should be more men teachers. 12. The distribution of qualified teachers should be equalized or inequalities compensated for. 13. Teachers in difficult schools should be paid more. 14. Competitiveness should be replaced by other incentives. 15. An analysis of curricula should be undertaken to enable learning to become meaningful and relevant. 16. Vocational training should be avoided. 17. Inappropriate teaching of grammar and language skills should be replaced by an exact study of deprived pupils' linguistic needs.

Some of Riessman's suggestions are open to criticism for two reasons: first he makes a number of unwarranted assumptions, for example, that 'culturally deprived' teachers would be more successful than others in dealing with culturally deprived children. There is no empirical justification for this belief: such teachers may, because of their own experiences and insecurity, be even more intolerant of lower-class culture than other teachers. Secondly Riessman never resolves a basic contradiction in his own approach: on the one hand he recommends accepting lower-class culture in its own right, accepting the non-verbal approach to life in such matters as psychotherapy, but at the same time he approves of introducing lower-class children to music and other experiences quite outside their normal cultural environment. Riessman, in other words, fails to make explicit a distinction between superficial cultural differences and differences in cultural background which will have profound experiential and cognitive effects. Thus he should have made clear that his second recommendation (about psychotherapy) would only be acceptable as a short term measure, and the same argument would apply to 'progressive education', etc.

Project Literacy

This was organized at Cornell University in February 1964 to study the specific problem of reading. However in its actual work-plans a much wider view of the problem of literacy has been taken:

> We believe that much current and potential research in learning psychology, visual perception, cognitive behaviour, neurophysiology of vision, child development, descriptive linguistics, psycho-linguistics, the sociology of educational innovation, research with culturally disadvantaged children and programme instruction . . . are essential to understanding literacy. Consequently, we are endeavouring to locate research interests which heretofor may not have been considered relevant to this crucial educational research area.

This project, directed by Professor H. Levin, is already producing interesting research reports on their plans and progress which are extremely relevant to the problems discussed above but they have appeared too recently for detailed report in this study. (Project Literacy Reports published by Cornell University, Ithaca, New York.)

Compensatory Education for Cultural Deprivation (Bloom, Davis and Hess, 1965.)

Following a conference held in Chicago in June 1964, a report was published which summarized the evidence regarding the nature of cultural deprivation and also made a series of recommendations for dealing with the problem (especially the U.S. problem). In addition a very useful annotated bibliography of relevant research was included in the report.

The recommendations of the conference are grouped in the following way:

1. *Basic needs.* Measures should be taken to ensure that pupils are adequately fed, clothed and medically cared for.

2. *Early Experience.* Nursery schools should be organized to provide stimulation of the kind that children from more favourable environments would have received at home. (This would include development of more 'extended' language.) Teachers in these nursery schools should be carefully selected and trained,

and parents should be involved in the school programme and ideally learn to develop their own range of communication.

3. *Elementary School.* Evidence should be obtained on each child at the beginning of the first grade to determine the levels he has reached with regard to perceptual development, language development, ability to attend, and motivation for learning. A variety of approaches to learning should be developed so that each child would be placed appropriately in the most rewarding setting. Classes at this stage should be small—preferably less than twenty—and the emphasis should be on the individual development of each child towards clear-cut tasks and goals. Once again language should play a considerable part in the programme.

4. *Adolescent Education.* Every effort should be made to identify deprived students with education: special instructional programmes, tutorial help and counselling should be offered; and attempts should be made to make use of peer societies to perform useful social functions.

Many of these recommendations have been incorporated into the research and intervention programme mounted by Professor R. Hess in Chicago.

Institute for Developmental Studies, New York

Perhaps the most ambitious and comprehensive programme yet to appear in the United States is the project reported by Martin Deutsch in 'Reversing Deprivation Effects in Pre-School Children' (1963). Acting on the existing evidence that children who are exposed to a greater variety of language patterns will be more likely to develop verbal skills, Deutsch set up a pre-school enrichment programme and proposed to investigate six specific areas: (a) the most appropriate kind of 'therapeutic' curriculum; (b) the academic success of such a programme with deprived children; (c) the social success of such a programme; (d) to investigate which ability patterns would be most affected by this kind of curriculum; (e) the training of teachers to deal with deprived children; (f) parent-school inter-action. This research is still in progress but after one year encouraging differences between the experimental (i.e. special programme) group and the control groups were observed.

Project Head Start

In October 1964 U.S. Congress passed the Economic Opportunity Act which was designed to minimize the impact of poverty and to attempt to eliminate it. Project Head Start was part of this general programme. Apart from its concern with early childhood education, the project, which was officially inaugurated in July 1965, integrated a comprehensive programme of improving children's health and nutrition: existing social services were to be utilized, parents were to be involved as much as possible, and volunteer helpers recruited as well as teachers. The project was designed to encourage communities to take responsibility for poverty and to develop programmes locally, the Office of Economic Opportunity merely being responsible for advising and ensuring that the academic nature of the educational programme was adequate.

The early childhood education consisted of pre-school 'deprived' children being admitted to 'child development centres' for an eight-week session in the summer prior to initial schooling. Drazek (1966) reports on the training of the 30,000 Head Start teachers which was undertaken by 118 colleges and universities all over the U.S.A. in May to June 1965. No uniform programme was developed, but Osborn (1966) states that the operation in most centres consisted of art, stories, science activities, creative play and visits to various community facilities: 'Many situations which the middle-class children take for granted Head Start children experienced for the first time. Many of these youngsters had never had a book read to them ...' However, Osborn's opinion was that possibly the biggest contribution of the project was to the teacher: firstly in alerting the teacher to the needs of the poor; secondly causing the teacher to realize that some progress was possible with such children in an eight-week period; and thirdly bringing about the commitment of the teacher to follow up the progress of the pupils in their initial schooling. Osborn's criticism of the project in some districts was that teachers had failed to take advantage of the extremely favourable teacher-pupil ratio (1 : 15, and with volunteers included an adult-child ratio of 1 : 5), and still regimented the children, not allowing them the degree of 'enrichment' that would have been possible under such circumstances even in a limited eight-week period.

A general report on the first session of the project was given by its Director, Mr. J. B. Richmond (1966), who suggested that the main lessons learnt in 1965 had been that communities possessed a great capacity to mobilize resources and staff in a very short time, and secondly that it was possible to recruit volunteer help.

These lessons might also be found to apply to Great Britain. On the other hand the main drawback of Project Head Start from a British point of view would be its lack of theoretical orientation: the impression is given in these reports that a great deal of time, money and energy is being expended without a clear analysis on the problem having been made and without clear objectives being defined.

PROGRAMMES IN GREAT BRITAIN

The Newsom Report

Perhaps the most obvious sign that the kind of research discussed in previous chapters has received official recognition was contained in the 'foreword' to the *Newsom Report* (Half Our Future, 1963) by the Minister of Education at that time, Sir Edward Boyle: 'All children should have an equal opportunity of acquiring intelligence, and of developing their talents and abilities to the full.'

The Report itself also reflected the results of recent research: apart from the general point about the inadequacy of resources, accommodation and teachers catering for the 'average and below average child', the committee focused particular attention in an early chapter (Chapter II) onto linguistic factors affecting pupils' achievement:

Employers complain not only of poor attainments but of the inadequate speech and inability of boys and girls to manage their dealings with other people. 'It is not so much that they are ill-mannered but that many of them have a complete lack of any social skill.' Other contributors to evidence write to us: 'We feel bound to record our impression that very many of these less gifted young people are socially maladroit, ill at ease in personal relationships, unduly self-regarding and insensitive; their contact even with their peers is often ineffectual; they understandably resent being organized by adults but show little gift for organizing themselves.' These are serious criticisms, certainly not applicable to all our pupils, but not either, easily to be dismissed. This matter of communication affects all aspects of social and intellectual growth. There is a gulf between those who have, and the many who have not, sufficient command of words to be able to listen and discuss rationally; to express ideas and feelings clearly; and even to have any ideas at all. We simply do not know how many people are frustrated in their lives by inability ever to express themselves adequately; or how many never develop intellectually because they lack the words with which to think and to reason. . . . The evidence of research increasingly suggests that linguistic inadequacy, disadvantages in social and physical background, and poor attainments in school, are closely associated. Because the forms of speech which are all they ever require for daily use in their homes and the neighbourhood in which they live are restricted, some boys and girls may never acquire the basic needs of learning and their intellectual potential is therefore masked. . . . If this is so, then here is a problem which can be tackled educationally although research and extensive experiment will be needed to discover the right teaching techniques.

On the basis of evidence which had been presented to the Committee they made the following recommendation:

There is an urgent need for research into the problems of environmental and linguistic handicaps, and of experiment in teaching techniques for overcoming the learning difficulties they create.

Later in the Report, when discussing the training of teachers, the Committee made this suggestion:

Such work as has been done in the study of social and environmental influences suggests that the learning difficulties, including the linguistic, of many of the pupils with whom we are concerned can be related to home background. And for some pupils the relation would seem to be very close indeed. Much investigation remains to be done, both in establishing the nature of the educational difficulties and in developing teaching techniques for dealing with them; we believe experiment in teaching techniques, based on the findings of research, is needed, and that some of this might best be undertaken by a training college in association with a specially-staffed experimental school. Apart, however, from these special enquiries all teachers in training should have some introduction to sociological study, such as many colleges now offer, in order that they may put their own job into social perspective and be better prepared to understand the difficulties of pupils in certain types of area.

The recommendation that an experimental school should be set up has not yet been adopted, but partly as a result of the Committee's recommendation, funds were made available to the *Sociological Research Unit* at the University of London Institute of Education. The project directed by Professor Basil Bernstein was designed (1) to investigate the exact nature of linguistic differences and their educational consequences among children from a lower working-class background, (2) to relate these language differences to differences in family structure and inter-action and (3) to mount an experimental intervention programme to extend the range of communication of these children in the first three years of their school life.

It is as yet too early to report on any results from this research but there are already indications that considerable progress will be made both in detailed analysis of the existing problem and in suggestions for intervention programmes.

The Plowden Report
In 1967 the Plowden Committee submitted its Report on

Children and Their Primary Schools. The terms of reference of the Committee were very wide—'To consider the whole subject of primary education and the transition to secondary education'. The Report was therefore only partly concerned with the problem discussed in this book, but even so many might consider that the question of language, social class and education was given much less attention than it warranted. Nevertheless on the general question of 'deprived' children the Report makes a number of unexceptional recommendations:

1. That there should be 'positive discrimination' in the financing and organization of primary schools: those schools in 'educational priority areas' or 'deprived' areas should have a *more* favourable pupil-teacher ratio so that no class should exceed thirty, and that good experienced teachers should be encouraged to undertake this kind of work by payment of additional salary. Teachers' aides, priority in new buildings, extra books and equipment were also recommended as urgent requirements.

2. The Committee recommended an expansion of nursery education especially for the 'priority' areas.

3. Colleges of Education should be more closely linked with the deprived areas, with the aim both of enriching the education of their students and of benefiting the schools.

4. In-service training should be expanded, and teachers' centres in priority areas should be set up to organize courses.

5. Attempts should be made to diversify the social compositions of the districts at present regarded as deprived.

6. All schools should have a programme for contact with children's parents.

These are very useful recommendations, but in many respects the Report is unsatisfactory and a number of criticisms both general and particular must be levelled against it:

1. Too much of the Report was psychological in orientation rather than sociological: for example, much is made of the importance of parents' attitudes, and how vital these are for the children, but no real attempt was made to account for the social origins of such attitudes. To encourage contact between parents

153

and schools is laudable, but only as a starting point—it is also necessary for teachers to be able to understand the cultural background of parents and to be able to communicate with them.

2. Few would argue with the recommendation that students at Colleges of Education should be brought into contact with the deprived areas schools, but the Report does not give adequate guidance on what parts students would play, or how they could be trained to cope with the problems of such schools.

3. There are a number of useful suggestions to teachers on the curriculum of the primary school, but many will think that the Report goes further in the direction of 'interest dominated' learning than the evidence of research justified. The 'free day' kind of organization may well be dangerous for some working-class children whose culture may not equip them with 'natural curiosity' to the same extent as those middle-class children the Report seems to regard as normal.

4. On the specific question of language there is a lack of clear perspective, and what appears to be a contradiction occurs. In a section headed 'Language' the following statement was made:

> Most children can make sentences by the time they go to school and are able to understand simple instructions given by unfamiliar people. Nevertheless, there will be a proportion who, because of difficulties in development or unfavourable backgrounds, are likely to lack fluency or have difficulty in making themselves understood. The psychological trauma of placing a child without adequate powers of communication in a new social situation can be serious. (Paragraph 55.)

No suggestions for coping with this 'trauma' are made, and later in the Report it is assumed that what 'culturally deprived' children need is simply 'perfectly normal, good primary schools alive with experience from which children of all kind can benefit'. In fact the chapter on the growth and development of children, although excellent in many respects, concludes with advice to teachers which I would regard as positively dangerous, especially if applied to the linguistic development of working-class children: 'Until a child is ready to take a particular step forward, it is a waste of time to try to teach him to take it.'

(Paragraph 75). I realize, of course, the theory behind this statement but surely its *unqualified* inclusion in an official Report is to be regretted.

Despite these criticisms, it is to be hoped that most of the Plowden Committee's recommendations will eventually be implemented; this will provide a beginning for a programme of reform—but much of the theoretical work needs to be completed, and more definite practical suggestions made.

VIII

CONCLUSION

This study began as a limited socio-linguistic analysis designed to throw some light on a social-educational problem. I found, however, that in order to answer many of the questions that arose during the course of this work, and in order to deal with problems of method and theory, a more extensive review of the literature in various fields became necessary.

The demographic evidence on the problem of educational opportunity was clear from the start, thus in Chapter I it was only necessary briefly to outline the evidence which has been frequently summarized elsewhere. However, the complex set of processes underlying the demographic indices relating to educational 'failure' needed analysis: I felt that it was important (in Chapter II) to examine the problem of working-class underachieving in education from the point of view of sub-cultural differences in motivation, attitudes to education, and cognitive processes. There is a great deal of evidence on these topics but it is extremely varied in quality, and therefore had to be critically evaluated as well as interpreted for the particular purpose of this book. By the end of Chapter II the focus of attention had already fixed upon the importance of language in educational processes and the effect this had for various social class groups in Great Britain. Chapter III had three purposes: first to examine previous studies to find out exactly what linguistic differences had been discovered between middle-class and working-class children at various ages; secondly to relate these differences to the environmental background wherever possible; and finally to see what kinds of linguistic measures had been found useful in the past. I found that the more recent studies of children's language and environment had tended to move away from simple linguistic counts in order to investigate kinds of thinking—in particular the terms 'abstract' and 'concrete' thinking were being used. Chapter IV Part I was therefore intended to examine the psychological literature bearing upon this question, in particular looking at the difficult question of the language and thought relationship, in an attempt to assess the importance of linguistic differences which exist between social groups, i.e. to examine the cognitive consequences of using different kinds of language. Chapter IV Part II looked at the same problem from the point of view of the social anthropological studies, examining not only the question of linguistic relativity but also wider questions of language, thought and culture, especially any of the theoretical work which would be relevant to Bernstein's theory which was examined next in Chapter V.

As a result of studying these inter-related fields, and the experimental work contained in Chapter VI, the following conclusions are tentatively made:

1. There is little doubt that there exists a social-educational problem: a great deal of potential talent is being wasted, or looking at the problem from a different point of view, the education of large numbers of working-class children is below a satisfactory standard. There is evidence to support the view that inadequacy of linguistic range and control is a very important factor in this under-achievement, and that linguistic inadequacy is a 'cumulative deficit' i.e. it is a disadvantage which generates a vicious circle of difficulties increasing in magnitude as school life progresses.

2. These linguistic difficulties are closely related to wider questions of 'motivation' and culture. To see the problem simply as language is inadequate, for language use is a translation of a culture through a specific social structure.

3. Some language differences facilitate certain kinds of expression—i.e. they make possible the explicit communication of certain modes of thought. Although it is generally accepted that 'Anything could be said in any language' it is still unquestionably the case that it is easier to say some things in some languages. Whether it can be said that language is a *determiner* of

perception, cognition and thought might be disputed, but there it little doubt that it exerts a channelling influence on thought processes. To ask whether language is a primary or secondary influence is less important than to think of the reciprocal relations between language and culture, language and social structure, language and cognition. Clearly individuals can form relations between phenomena without the mediation or the control of language, but evidence indicates that the character and range of such relations are limited. It would be wrong, however, to give the impression that culture is transmitted only by language: socialization into the culture is effected through a range of channels, verbal and extra-verbal.

4. It could be argued that the 1944 Education Act or the more recent moves to make secondary education comprehensive were attempts to modify social structure. Such measures can have only limited success unless conscious attempts are also made to provide opportunities for the extension of linguistic facility within the educational institutions.

5. The most constructive approach to the last point would be to see the problem as a set of inter-related difficulties of cultural discontinuity and code-learning. Sociologists are becoming increasingly interested in the fact that the difficulty of working-class children adjusting to school is a problem of discontinuity— they come to school with attitudes, values and expectations (acquired in the process of being socialized into a working-class sub-culture) which are very different from the values of the middle-class culture of the school. This is a problem in itself, but it also poses very difficult questions relating to the problems of code learning. If Bernstein's view of context, role, culture and language is accepted, then code learning, or extending pupils' range of control over language, must be achieved through changes in the social structure of the school, through extended possibilities of developing new role-relations. The actual social organization of the school to make this kind of learning possible is one difficulty; another is that some teachers may feel that it is not morally or socially right to 'interfere' with a pupil's way of life in this fashion. These qualms of conscience may be praise-worthy, but logically they are unsound for the following reasons:

(a) Any form of teaching is to some extent an 'intrusion' or 'interference'.

(b) What is being suggested is what most philosophers of education would regard as a central aim in education: i.e. controlled and disciplined extension of experience. It is however important to stress the notion of extension rather than replacement.

(c) Schools are already attempting to transform their pupils into middle-class children, but they are often focusing upon the 'wrong' aspects of middle-class culture—sometimes with very unfortunate results (see Jackson and Marsden, 1962). What is here suggested is that teachers should become more sensitive to the kind of analysis which would enable them to distinguish in the so-called middle-class culture what is of cognitive importance from what is irrelevant to the educational process. Far too often it seems that schools are emphasizing trivial aspects of middle-class life (such as etiquette and social conventions) and neglecting important cognitive areas.

It is very important that a sentimental attitude towards working-class language be avoided. Undoubtedly it possesses a certain dramatic vigour and colour which should be preserved. But it should also be recognized that such language forms are in some important respects limited in range and control. The sentimental attitude to working-class language is only one expression of a falsely romantic view of working-class life in general: apart from the argument outlined above—that the educational aim must be extension of experience rather than a 'conversion' process—there is the simple socio-economic fact that traditional working-class socialization processes are preparing its young members for a world which is disappearing: in the near future routine manual jobs are going to disappear and jobs which will become available in industry or in bureaucratic, welfare or distribution spheres will require a much higher level of symbolic control.

6. If the extension of the range of role relationships and opportunities for code learning are accepted as educational aims, a great deal of attention will have to be paid to appropriate

methods of role learning and code learning, but in all cases the important factor should be that teachers should never give the impression to a working-class child that his culture in general, or his form of speech in particular is in any way inferior to the culture of the school. The concept of appropriateness rather than right or wrong speech and behaviour should become the desired end. It will, however, be important for teachers to avoid the danger of teaching language simply as a skill.

7. Another difficulty that follows from the above argument is that it will become increasingly clear that only a limited amount of success will be possible within the school without at least passive co-operation of the parents of working-class children. If it is accepted that it is important to bridge the gap between school and home, it will have to be decided what are the best means of doing this; whether it is a task for experienced teachers or head teachers and their assistants, or whether it is a task to be delegated to specially trained social workers attached to the schools. What seems to be required is that the school must not insulate itself from the home and community but must work out areas of action for parents that they *can* perform and which lead to immediate success.

8. All this work needs adequately trained staff, but an additional difficulty here, as with the problem of research into this area is that it requires a multi-disciplinary approach, and in this country sociologists are usually without any linguistic training and also it is traditionally difficult for sociologists and psychologists to see problems from the point of view of the other discipline. The training of staff therefore will be a major difficulty.

9. The kind of programme outlined above may well require changes in the social structure and the culture of the school, more sensitive training of teachers, and re-assessment of the curriculum. It may also be the case, from evidence of research in the United States, that far more attention should be paid to curriculum teaching method. It seems strange that there has as yet been no systematic approach to this problem, although a number of isolated attempts have been made.

10. Much more fundamental questions are raised by the approach taken in this study: for example it raises the question as to what is the meaning of educational success in a democratic

society over and above examination success. Social participation in such societies requires of individuals a much higher level of critical awareness both of the nature of the society and their own relation to it.

BIBLIOGRAPHY

ADAMS, S. (1938) 'Analysis of verb forms in the speech of young children', *J. Exp. Educ.* 7.

ALDRICH, C. A., NORVAL, M., and KNOP, C. (1946) 'The crying of newly born babies', *J. Pediat.* 28.

ALDRICH, C. A., SUNG, C., and KNOP, C. (1945) 'The crying of newborn babies', *J. Pediat.* 27.

AMES, L. D. (1946) 'The development of the sense of time in the child', *J. Genet. Psychol.* 68.

ANANIEV, B. G. (1955) 'The basis of spatial discrimination', in Simon, B. (1957), London and New York.

BANTOCK, G. H. (1964) *Education and Values*. London.

BAYLEY, N. (1933) *Mental growth during the first three years*. Genet. Psychol. Monograph 14. No. 1.

BEAN, C. H. (1932) 'An unusual opportunity to investigate the psychology of language', *J. Genet. Psychol.* 40.

BERNSTEIN, B. B. (1958) 'Some sociological determinants of perception', *B. J. Sociology* 9.

— (1959) 'A public language: some sociological determinants of linguistic form', *B. J. Sociology* 10.

— (1960) 'Language and social class', *B. J. Sociology* 11.

— (1961) a. 'Social structure, language and learning', *Educ. Research* 3.

— (1961) b. 'Social class and linguistic development: a theory of social learning', in *Economy, Education and Society*, ed. by Halsey, A. H., Floud, J. and Anderson, C. A., New York.

— (1961) c. 'Aspects of language and learning in the genesis of the social process', *J. of Child Psychol. and Psychiat.* 1.

— (1962) a. 'Linguistic codes, hesitation phenomena and intelligence', *Language and Speech* 5.

— (1962) b. 'Social class, linguistic codes and grammatical elements', *Language and Speech* 5.

— (1964) 'Family role systems, socialization and communication'. Paper given at the Conference on Cross-Cultural Research into Childhood and Adolescence. Chicago.

— (1965) 'A socio-linguistic approach to social learning', in *Social Science Survey*, ed. by Gould, J. London.

BLATS, W. E., FLETCHER, M. I., and MASON, M. (1937) 'Collected studies on the Dionne Quintuplets', Univ. Toronto Stud. Child Development. Ser. No. 16.

BLOOM, B. S., DAVIS, A., and HESS, R. (1965) *Compensatory Education for Cultural Deprivation*. New York.

BLOOMFIELD, L. (1927) 'Literate and illiterate speech', in Hymes (1964).

BORELLI, M. (1951) 'The performance of deaf and hearing children on serial ordering tasks', *Enfance* 4.

BOTT, E. (1957) *Family and Social Network*. London and New York.

BRAIN, R. (1962) 'Speech and its disorders: the physiological basis of speech', *Advancement of Science*, Vol. 19, No. 79.

BROADBENT, D. E. (1959) 'Review of "Verbal Behaviour" by B. F. Skinner', *B. J. of Psychol.* 50, 4.

BRODBECK, A. J., and IRWIN, O. C. (1946) 'The speech behaviour of infants without families', *Child Development* 17.

BRONFENBRENNER, U. (1958) 'Socialization and social class through time and space', in *Readings in Social Psychology*, ed. by Maccoby, E. E.

BROWN, R. W., and LENNEBERG, E. H. (1954) 'A study in language and cognition', *J. Abn. and Soc. Psychol.* 49.

BRUNER, J. S. (1964) 'The Course of Cognitive Growth', *American Psychologist*, 19, 1–15.

— et al. (1966) *Studies in Cognitive Growth*. New York.

BUHLER, C. (1931) *Kindheit und Jugend*. Leipzig.

BULL, W. (1955) 'The use of vernacular language in fundamental education', in Hymes (1964).

BURT, C. (1945) 'The education of illiterate adults', *B. J. Educ. Psychol.* XV.

CARROLL, J. B., and CASAGRANDE, J. B. (1958) 'The function of language classifications in behaviour', in *Readings in Social Psychology*, ed. by Maccoby *et al.* London.

CARROLL, J. B. (1938) Diversity of vocabulary and the harmonic series of word frequency distribution. *Psychol. Rec.* 2.

CARROLL, J. B. (1964) *Language and Thought.* Englewood Cliffs, N. J.

CHAMBERLAIN, A. F. (1900) *The Child: A Study in the Evolution of Man.* New York.

CHOMSKY, N. (1957) *Syntactic Structures.* The Hague and New York.

— (1959) 'Review of "Verbal Behaviour" by B. F. Skinner', *Language* 35.

CHULLIAT, R., and OLÉRON, P. (1955) The role of language in transposition tasks. *Enfance* 8.

CHURCH, J. (1961) *Language and the Discovery of Reality.* New York.

CLARKE, A. M., and CLARKE, A. D. B. (eds.) (1958) *Mental Deficiency: the Changing Outlook.* London.

Committee on Higher Education (1963) *Higher Education* (The Robbins Report). London.

CONKLIN, H. C. (1955) 'Hanunoo Color Categories', in Hymes (1964).

DAVIS, A. (1948) *Social Class Influences on Learning.* Cambridge, Massachusetts.

— and HAVIGHURST, R. J. (1946) 'Social class and color differences in child rearing', *Am. Soc. Rev.* XI.

DAVIS, E. A. (1937) *The development of linguistic skill in twins, singletons with siblings and only children from age 5 to 10 years.* Institute of Child Welfare. Monograph Ser. No. 14.

DAWE, H. C. (1942) 'A study of the effect of an educational programme upon language development', *J. Exp. Educ.* 11.

DAY, E. J. (1932) 'The development of language in twins', *Child Development* 3.

DENNIS, M., HENRIQUES, F., and SLAUGHTER, C. (1956) *Coal is our Life.* London.

DESCOEUDRES, A. (1921) *Le Développement de l'Enfant de deux à sept ans.* Heuchztel et Paris.

DEUTSCH, M. P. (1963) 'Reversing deprivation effects in pre-school children'. Mimeograph. Institute for Developmental Studies. New York Medical College.

— (1963) 'The disadvantaged child and the learning process', in Passow, H. *Education in Depressed Areas.* New York.

— MALIVER, A., BROWN, D. and CHERRY, E. (1964) 'Communication of information in the elementary school classroom'.

Mimeograph. Institute for Developmental Studies. New York Medical College.

DEUTSCH, M. P. (1964) 'The role of social class in language development and cognition'. Mimeograph. Annual Meeting Ortho-psych. Association.

DOUGLAS, J. W. B. (1964) *The Home and the School*. London and New York.

DOWNES, D. M. (1966) *The Delinquent Solution*. London.

DRAZEK, S. J. (1966) 'Training 30,000 Head Start teachers', *School and Society* 94.

ESTOUP, J, B. (1917) *Gammes Sténographiques*. Paris.

EWING, A. W. C. (ed.) (1957) *Educational Guidance and the Deaf Child*, Manchester.

FERGUSON, C. A. (1959) 'Diglossia', in Hymes (1964).

FIRTH, J. R. (1935) 'On sociological linguistics', in Hymes (1964).

— (1950) 'Personality and language in society', *Sociological Review* 42.

FISCHELLI, R. M. (1950) 'A study of prelinguistic speech development of institutionalized infants'. Ph.D. Fordham.

FISHER, M. S. (1932) *Language patterns of pre-school children*. Child Development Monograph No. 15.

FISHMAN, J. A. (1960) 'A systematization of the Whorfian hypothesis', *Behavioral Science* 5.

FLAVELL, J. H. (1963) *The developmental Psychology of Jean Piaget*. Princeton, N.J.

FLOUD, J. E., HALSEY, A. H., and MARTIN, F. M. (1956) *Social Class and Educational Opportunity*. London.

FRAKE, C. O. (1961) 'The diagnosis of disease among the Subanum of Mindanao', in Hymes (1964).

GASTIL, R. D. (1959) 'Relative linguistic determinism'. *Anthropol Linguistics* 1, No. 9.

GESELL, A. (1925) *The Mental Growth of the Pre-School Child*. New York

GOLDFARB, W. (1943) a. 'Infant Rearing and Problem Behaviour'. *American Journal of Orthopsychiatry* 13.

— (1943) b. 'The effects of early institutional care on adolescent personality', *J. Exp. Educ.* 12.

— (1945) 'Effects on psychological deprivation in infancy

and subsequent stimulation'. *American Journal of Psychology* 102.

GOLDMAN-EISLER, F. (1954) 'On the variability of the speed of talking and on its relation to the length of utterances in conversations', *Brit. J. Psychol.*, 45, 94.

— (1961) a. 'Continuity of speech utterance, its determinants and its significance', *Language and Speech* 2.

GOLDMAN-EISLER, F. (1961) b. 'Hesitation and information in speech', in *Proceedings of 4th London Symposium on Information Theory*.

GOODENOUGH, F. L. (1938) 'The use of pronouns by young children: a note on the development of self-awareness', *J. Genet. Psychol.* 52.

GOTTLIEB, D., and REEVES, J. (1963) *Adolescent Behavior in Urban Areas*. New York.

GRAY, J. L., and MOSHINSKY, P. (1938) 'Ability and Opportunity in English Education', in Hogben, L. *Political Arithmetic*. London.

GUMPERZ, J. (1961) 'Speech variation and the study of Indian civilization', in Hymes (1964).

— and HYMES, D. (eds.) (1964) 'The Ethnography of Communication', *American Anthropol.* Special Public. 66. (Dec. 1964).

HAHN, E. (1948) 'Analysis of the content and form of the speech of first grade children', *Quarterly Journal of Speech* 34.

HALLIDAY, M. A. K., MCINTOSH, A., and STREVENS, P. (1964) *The Linguistic Sciences and Language Teaching*. London.

HALSEY, A. H. (ed.) (1961) *Ability and Educational Opportunity*. O.E.C.D.

— and GARDNER, L. (1953) 'Selection for secondary education and achievement in four grammar schools', *Brit. J. Sociology* 4.

HARRELL, L. E. (1957) *A comparison of the development of oral and written language in school age children*. Monograph Society for Research in Child Development XXII, 66.

HARWOOD, F. W. (1959) 'Quantitative study of the syntax of the speech of Australian children', *Language and Speech* 2.

HEBB, D. O. (1949) *Organization of Behavior*. New York.

HEIDER, F. K., and HEIDER, G. M. (1940) *A comparison of sentence structure of deaf and hearing children*. Psychological Monograph 52, No. 1.

— (1941) *Studies in the psychology of the deaf*. Psychological Monograph 53.

HIMMELWEIT, H. (1954) 'Social Status and Secondary Education since the 1944 Act', in Glass, D. V. (ed.), *Social Mobility in Britain*. London and New York.

HOCKET, C. F. (1954) 'Chinese versus English', In Hoijer, H. (ed). *Language and Culture* (1954). Chicago.

HOGGART, R. (1957) *The Uses of Literacy*. London.

HOIJER, H. (1951) 'Cultural implications of some Navaho linguistic categories', *Language 27*.

— (ed.) (1954) *Language in Culture*. Chicago.

HOWARD, R. W. (1946) 'The Language development of a group of triplets,' *J. Genet. Psychol*. 69.

HUMPHREY, G. (1951) *Thinking*. London.

HUNT, J. MCV. (1961) *Intelligence and Experience*. New York.

HYMES, D. (ed.) (1964) *Language in Culture and Society*. New York.

IRWIN, O. C. (1948) 'Infant speech', *J. Speech and Hearing Disorders*, 13.

JACKSON, B., and MARSDEN, D. (1962) *Education and the Working Class*. London.

JESPERSON, O. (1924) *The Philosophy of Grammar*. London.

JOHN, V. P. (1962) *The intellectual development of slum children*. Annual Meeting American Orthopsychiatric Association.

KENDALL, D. C. (1953) 'The mental development of young deaf children', in Ewing (1957).

KERR, M. (1958) *People of Ship Street*. London.

KLEIN, J. (1965) *Samples from English Cultures*. London.

KOHN, M. L. (1959) a. 'Social class and parental values', *Am. J. Soc. Rev*. June.

— (1959) b. 'Social class and the exercise of parental authority', *Am. Soc. Rev*. June.

KOLBAYA, M. G. (1953) 'The Part Played by speech in the Thought Process', in O'Connor (1961).

KUENNE, M. R. (1946) 'Experimental investigation of the relation of language to transpositional behaviour in young children', *J. Exp. Psychol*. 36.

KURTZ, K. H., and HOVLAND, C. I. (1953) 'The effect of verbalization during observation of stimulus objects upon accuracy of recognition and recall', *J. Exp. Psychol.* 45.

LABRANT, L. L. (1933) *A study of certain language developments of children in grades 4 to 12 inclusive.* Genet. Psychol. Monograph 14.

LAWTON, D. (1963) 'Social class differences in language development: a study of some samples of written work', *Language and Speech* 6, Part 3.

— (1964) 'Social class language differences in group discussions', *Language and Speech* 7, Part 3.

— (1965) 'Social class language differences in individual interviews'. Mimeograph Sociological Research Unit, University of London Institute of Education.

— (1967) 'A study of linguistic differences in samples of the speech and writing of groups of working-class and middle-class boys aged twelve and fifteen'. Ph.D. London.

LEWIS, M. M. (1936) *Infant Speech.* London.

— (1951) *Infant Speech* (2nd Edition with additional chapters). London.

— (1953) *The Importance of Illiteracy.* London.

— (1963) *Language, Thought and Personality.* London and New York.

LINDEMAN, R. (1938) *Der Begrif der Conscience im Frazosichen Denken.* Quoted by Fishman, J. (1960).

LIUBLINSKAYA, A. A. (1957) 'The Development of Children's Speech and Thought', in Simon, B. (1957). London.

LOBAN, W. D. (1961) 'The Language of Elementary School Children'. Mimeograph.

— (1963) *The Language of Elementary School Children.* N.C.T.E. Research Report No. 1. Champaign, Illinois.

LOCKWOOD, D., and GOLDTHORPE, J. (1963) 'Affluence and the British Class Structure', *Sociological Review,* July 1963.

LURIA, A. R. (1955) 'The Role of Language in the Formation of Temporary Connections', in Simon, B. (1957). London.

— (1961) *The Role of Speech in the Regulation of Normal and Abnormal Behaviour.* London and New York.

— and YUDOVICH, I. (1959) *Speech and the Development of Mental Processes in the Child.* London and New York.

— and VINOGRADOVA, O. S. (1959) 'The synamics and semantic systems', *B. J. Psychol.* 50.

MALINOWSKI, B. (1923) 'The Problem of Meaning in Primitive Languages', in Ogden, C. K., and Richards, I. A. *The Meaning of Meaning*. London and New York.

— (1935) *Coral Gardens and Their Magic*. London and Bloomington, Indiana.

— (1937) 'The Dilemma of Contemporary Linguistics' (Review of M. M. Lewis Infant Speech). *Nature* 140.

MCCARTHY, D. M. (1930) *The Language Development of the Pre-School Child*. Inst. Child Welfare. Monograph No 4.

— (1954) 'Language Development in Children', in Carmichael, L. *Manual of Child Psychology*. New York.

MCCLELLAND, D. C., ATKINSON, J., CLARK, R. A., and LOWELL, B. L. (1953) *The Achievement Motive*. New York.

MCCLELLAND, D. C., BALDWIN, A. L., BRONFENBRENNER, U., and STRODBECK, F. L. (1958) *Talent and Society*. Princeton, N.J.

MCCLELLAND, D. C. (1961) *The Achieving Society*. Princeton, N.J.

MCNALLY, J., and MURRAY, W. (1962) *Key Words to Literacy: A Basic Word List*. London.

MILLER, G. A. (1951) *Language and Communication*. New York.

MILNER, E. (1951) 'A study of the relationships between reading readiness in grade 1 school children and patterns of parent child interaction', *Child Development* 22.

Ministry of Education, C.A.C.E. (1959) 15–18 (*The Crowther Report*) London.

— (1954) *Early Leaving Report*. London.

— (1963) *Half our Future*. (The Newsom Report). London.

MOGEY, J. (1956) *Family and Neighbourhood*. Oxford.

MOORE, J. K. (1947) 'Speech content of selected groups of orphanage and non-orphanage pre-school children', *J. Exp. Educ.* 16.

NATADZE, R. G. (1957) 'Studies on Thought and Speech Problems by Psychologists of the Georgian S.S.R.', in O'Connor (1961).

NEWMAN, S. (1955) 'Vocabulary Levels: Zuni Sacred and Slang Usage', in Hymes (1964).

NICE, M. M. (1933) 'A child's attainment of the sentence', *J. Genet. Psychol.* 42.

NISBET, J. (1953) 'Family Environment and Intelligence', in

Education, Economy and Society. Ed. by Halesy, A., H. Floud, J., and Anderson, C. A. (1691). New York.

O'CONNOR, N. (ed.) (1961) *Recent Soviet Psychology.* London and New York.

— and HERMELIN, B. (1963) *Speech and Thought in Severe Abnormality.* London and New York.

OLÉRON, P. (1957) *Recherches sur le développement mental des sourd-muets.* Paris.

OSBORN, D. K. (1966) 'A look at child development centres: Operation Head Start', *The Reading Teacher* 19.5.

OSGOOD, L. E. (1953) *Method and Theory in Experimental Psychology.* New York.

PASSOW, A. H. (1963) *Education in Depressed Areas.* New York, Teachers College Columbia.

PAVLOV, I. P. (1927) *Conditioned Reflexes: An Investigation of the Physiological Activity of the Cerebral Cortex.* Tr. and ed. by G. V. Anrep. London.

— (1928) *Lectures on Conditioned Reflexes.* Tr. and ed. by W. H. Gantt. London and New York.

— (1941) *Conditioned Reflexes and Psychiatry.* Tr. and ed. by W. H. Gantt. New York.

— (1955) *Selected Works.* Moscow and San Francisco.

PIAGET, J. (1926, Rev. ed. 1959) *Language and Thought of the Child.* London and New York.

— (1962) 'Comments on Vygotsky's critical remarks', in Vygotsky (1962). London and New York.

PIAGET, J., and INHELDER, B. (1958) *The Growth of Logical Thinking from Childhood to Adolescence.* New York.

PRANGISHVILI, A. S. (1954) 'Psychological Problems of the Development of Thought', in O'Connor (1961).

PRINGLE, M. L. KELLMER (1965) *Deprivation and Education.* London.

PRINGLE, M. L. KELLMER, and BOSSIO, V. (1958) 'A study of deprived children. Part I, Intellectual, emotional and social development', *Vita Humana* I.

— (1958) 'A study of deprived children. Part II, Language development and reading attainment', *Vita Humana* I.

— (1960) 'Early, prolonged separation and emotional maladjustment', *J. of Child Psychol. and Psychiatry* I.

PYLES, M. K. (1932) Verbalization as a factor in learning. *Child Development* 3.

RAVENETTE, T. (1963) 'Intelligence, Personality and Social Class: an investigation into the problems of intelligence and personality of working class secondary school children'. Ph.D. Thesis. London.

RICHMOND, J. B. (1966) 'Communities in Action: A Report on Project Head Start'. *The Reading Teacher* 19.5. (Feb.).

RIESSMAN, F. (1962) *The Culturally Deprived Child*. New York.

ROSEN, B. C. (1956) 'The Achievement Syndrome', *Am. Sociol. Rev.* 21.

ROUDINESCO, J., and APPELL, G. (1950) 'Les Répurcussions de la Stabulation Hôpitalière sur le Développement Psychomoteur des jeunes Enfants', *Semaine des Hôpiteaux*, Paris, 26.

SAMPSON, O. C. (1956) 'A study of speech development in children 18–30 months', *B. J. Educ. Psych.* 26.

— (1959) 'The speech and language development of 5-year-old children', *B. J. Educ. Psych.* 29.

SAPIR, E. (1921) *Language*. New York.

— (1961) 'Culture, Language and Personality', *Selected Essays* ed. by Mandelbaum, D. G., and Berkeley, L. A.

SCHNEIDER, L., and LYSGAARD, S. (1953) 'The deferred gratification pattern', *Am. Soc. Rev.* April.

SCHONELL, F. (1942) *Backwardness in the Basic Subjects*. Edinburgh.

SEWELL, W. H. (1961) 'Social class and childhood personality', *Sociometry* 24.

SHEPARD, W. O., and SCHAEFFER, M. (1956) 'The effect of concept knowledge on discrimination learning', *Child Development* 27.

SHIRE, M. L. (1945) 'The relation of certain linguistic factors to reading achievement in first grade children'. Ph.D. Fordham.

SHIRLEY, M. M. (1938) 'Common content in the speech of pre-school children', *Child Development* 9.

SIEGAL, S. (1956) *Non-parametric Statistics*. New York.

SILLER, J. (1957) 'Socio-economic status and conceptual thinking', *J. of Abn. and Soc. Psych.* Nov.

SIMON, B. (ed.) (1957) *Psychology in the Soviet Union*. London.

SKINNER, B. F. (1957) *Verbal Behaviour*. New York.

SMITH, A. G. (ed.) (1966) *Communication and Culture.* New York.

SMITH, M. E. (1926) 'An investigation of the development of the sentence and the extent of vocabulary in young children', *Univ. Iowa, Stud. Child Welfare* 3, No. 5.

— (1935) 'A study of some factors influencing the development of the sentence in pre-school children', *J. Genet. Psychol.* 46.

— (1939) 'Some light on the problem of bilingualism', Genet., Psychol. Monograph 21.

SPIKER, L., GERYNOY, J. R., and SHEPARD, W. O. (1956) 'Children's concepts of middle-sizedness and performance of the intermediate size problem', *J. Occ. Psychol.* 79.

SPINLEY, B. M. (1953) *The Deprived and the Privileged.* London and New York.

STRICKLAND, R. (1962) 'The language of elementary school children', *Bull. of School of Ed.* Vol. 38, No. 4.

SYMONDS, P. M., and DARINGER, H. F. (1930) 'Studies in the learning of English expression', *Teach. Coll. Rec.* 32.

TEMPLIN, M. C. (1957) *Certain Language skills in children.* Inst. of Child Welfare. Monog. No. 26.

TRAGER, G. L. (1959) 'The Systematization of the Whorfian hypothesis', *Anthrop. Ling.* 1. No. 1.

UZNADZE, D. N. (1927) 'The Internal Form of Speech', in O'Connor (1961).

VERNON, P. E. (1955) *The bearing of recent advances in psychology on educational problems.* Studies in Educ. No. 7. Univ. London. Institute of Education.

VINCENT, M. (1957) 'The performance of deaf and hearing children on a classifying task', *Enfance* 10.

VYGOTSKY, L. S. (1962) *Thought and Language.* London and Cambridge, Massachusetts.

WEIR, M. W., and STEPHENSON, H. W. (1959) 'The effects of verbalization in children's learning', *Child Development* 30.

WHORF, B. L. (1956) *Language, Thought and Reality.* Ed. by Carroll, J. B. New York and Cambridge, Massachusetts.

WILLIAMS, H. M. (1937) *An analytic study of language achievement in pre-school children.* Univ. Iowa. Stud. Child Welfare, 13, No. 2.

— and MCFARLAND, M. L. (1937) *Development of language and vocabulary in young children.* Univ. Iowa. Stud. Child Welfare, 13, No. 2.

YOUNG, F. M. (1941) *An analysis of certain variables in a developmental study of language.* Genet. Psychol. Monograph 23.

ZATKIS, J. (1949) 'The effect of the need for achievement on linguistic behaviour', in McClelland *et al.*, *The Achievement Motive* (1953). New York.

INDEX OF AUTHORS

INDEX OF SUBJECTS

The International Library of
Sociology
and Social Reconstruction

Edited by W. J. H. SPROTT
Founded by KARL MANNHEIM

ROUTLEDGE & KEGAN PAUL
BROADWAY HOUSE, CARTER LANE, LONDON, E.C.4

CONTENTS

PRINTED IN GREAT BRITAIN BY HEADLEY BROTHERS LTD
109 KINGSWAY LONDON WC2 AND ASHFORD KENT

GENERAL SOCIOLOGY

Brown, Robert. Explanation in Social Science. *208 pp. 1963. (2nd Impression 1964.) 25s.*

Gibson, Quentin. The Logic of Social Enquiry. *240 pp. 1960. (3rd Impression 1968.) 24s.*

Homans, George C. Sentiments and Activities: Essays in Social Science. *336 pp. 1962. 32s.*

Isajiw, Wsevelod W. Causation and Functionalism in Sociology. *165 pp. 1968. 25s.*

Johnson, Harry M. Sociology: a Systematic Introduction. *Foreword by Robert K. Merton. 710 pp. 1961. (5th Impression 1968.) 42s.*

Mannheim, Karl. Essays on Sociology and Social Psychology. *Edited by Paul Keckskemeti. With Editorial Note by Adolph Lowe. 344 pp. 1953. (2nd Impression 1966.) 32s.*

Systematic Sociology: An Introduction to the Study of Society. *Edited by J. S. Erös and Professor W. A. C. Stewart. 220 pp. 1957. (3rd Impression 1967.) 24s.*

Martindale, Don. The Nature and Types of Sociological Theory. *292 pp. 1961. (3rd Impression 1967.) 35s.*

Maus, Heinz. A Short History of Sociology. *234 pp. 1962. (2nd Impression 1965.) 28s.*

Myrdal, Gunnar. Value in Social Theory: A Collection of Essays on Methodology. *Edited by Paul Streeten. 332 pp. 1958. (3rd Impression 1968.) 35s.*

Ogburn, William F., and Nimkoff, Meyer F. A Handbook of Sociology. *Preface by Karl Mannheim. 656 pp. 46 figures. 35 tables. 5th edition (revised) 1964. 45s.*

Parsons, Talcott, and Smelser, Neil J. Economy and Society: A Study in the Integration of Economic and Social Theory. *362 pp. 1956. (4th Impression 1967.) 35s.*

Rex, John. Key Problems of Sociological Theory. *220 pp. 1961. (4th Impression 1968.) 25s.*

Stark, Werner. The Fundamental Forms of Social Thought. *280 pp. 1962. 32s.*

FOREIGN CLASSICS OF SOCIOLOGY

Durkheim, Emile. Suicide. A Study in Sociology. *Edited and with an Introduction by George Simpson. 404 pp. 1952. (4th Impression 1968.) 35s.*

Professional Ethics and Civic Morals. *Translated by Cornelia Brookfield. 288 pp. 1957. 30s.*

Gerth, H. H., and Mills, C. Wright. From Max Weber: Essays in Sociology. *502 pp. 1948. (6th Impression 1967.) 35s.*

Tönnies, Ferdinand. Community and Association. *(Gemeinschaft und Gesellschaft.) Translated and Supplemented by Charles P. Loomis. Foreword by Pitirim A. Sorokin. 334 pp. 1955. 28s.*

3

SOCIAL STRUCTURE

Andreski, Stanislav. Military Organization and Society. *Foreword by Professor A. R. Radcliffe-Brown. 226 pp. 1 folder. 1954. Revised Edition 1968. 35s.*

Cole, G. D. H. Studies in Class Structure. *220 pp. 1955. (3rd Impression 1964.) 21s. Paper 10s. 6d.*

Coontz, Sydney H. Population Theories and the Economic Interpretation. *202 pp. 1957. (3rd Impression 1968.) 28s.*

Coser, Lewis. The Functions of Social Conflict. *204 pp. 1956. (3rd Impression 1968.) 25s.*

Dickie-Clark, H. F. Marginal Situation: A Sociological Study of a Coloured Group. *240 pp. 11 tables. 1966. 40s.*

Glass, D. V. (Ed.). Social Mobility in Britain. *Contributions by J. Berent, T. Bottomore, R. C. Chambers, J. Floud, D. V. Glass, J. R. Hall, H. T. Himmelweit, R. K. Kelsall, F. M. Martin, C. A. Moser, R. Mukherjee, and W. Ziegel. 420 pp. 1954. (4th Impression 1967.) 45s.*

Jones, Garth N. Planned Organizational Change: An Exploratory Study Using an Empirical Approach. *About 268 pp. 1969. 40s.*

Kelsall, R. K. Higher Civil Servants in Britain: From 1870 to the Present Day. *268 pp. 31 tables. 1955. (2nd Impression 1966.) 25s.*

König, René. The Community. *232 pp. Illustrated. 1968. 35s.*

Lawton, Denis. Social Class, Language and Education. *192 pp. 1968. (2nd Impression 1968.) 25s.*

McLeish, John. The Theory of Social Change: Four Views Considered. *About 128 pp. 1969. 21s.*

Marsh, David C. The Changing Social Structure in England and Wales, 1871-1961. *1958. 272 pp. 2nd edition (revised) 1966. (2nd Impression 1967.) 35s.*

Mouzelis, Nicos. Organization and Bureaucracy. An Analysis of Modern Theories. *240 pp. 1967. (2nd Impression 1968.) 28s.*

Ossowski, Stanislaw. Class Structure in the Social Consciousness. *210 pp. 1963. (2nd Impression 1967.) 25s.*

SOCIOLOGY AND POLITICS

Barbu, Zevedei. Democracy and Dictatorship: Their Psychology and Patterns of Life. *300 pp. 1956. 28s.*

Crick, Bernard. The American Science of Politics: Its Origins and Conditions. *284 pp. 1959. 32s.*

Hertz, Frederick. Nationality in History and Politics: A Psychology and Sociology of National Sentiment and Nationalism. *432 pp. 1944. (5th Impression 1966.) 42s.*

Kornhauser, William. The Politics of Mass Society. *272 pp. 20 tables. 1960. (3rd Impression 1968.) 28s.*

Laidler, Harry W. History of Socialism. Social-Economic Movements: An Historical and Comparative Survey of Socialism, Communism, Co-operation, Utopianism; and other Systems of Reform and Reconstruction. *New edition. 992 pp. 1968. 90s.*

Lasswell, Harold D. Analysis of Political Behaviour. An Empirical Approach. *324 pp. 1947. (4th Impression 1966.) 35s.*

Mannheim, Karl. Freedom, Power and Democratic Planning. *Edited by Hans Gerth and Ernest K. Bramstedt. 424 pp. 1951. (3rd Impression 1968.) 42s.*

Mansur, Fatma. Process of Independence. *Foreword by A. H. Hanson. 208 pp. 1962. 25s.*

Martin, David A. Pacificism: an Historical and Sociological Study. *262 pp. 1965. 30s.*

Myrdal, Gunnar. The Political Element in the Development of Economic Theory. *Translated from the German by Paul Streeten. 282 pp. 1953. (4th Impression 1965.) 25s.*

Polanyi, Michael. F.R.S. The Logic of Liberty: Reflections and Rejoinders. *228 pp. 1951. 18s.*

Verney, Douglas V. The Analysis of Political Systems. *264 pp. 1959. (3rd Impression 1966.) 28s.*

Wootton, Graham. The Politics of Influence: British Ex-Servicemen, Cabinet Decisions and Cultural Changes, 1917 to 1957. *316 pp. 1963. 30s.*
Workers, Unions and the State. *188 pp. 1966. (2nd Impression 1967.) 25s.*

FOREIGN AFFAIRS: THEIR SOCIAL, POLITICAL AND ECONOMIC FOUNDATIONS

Baer, Gabriel. Population and Society in the Arab East. *Translated by Hanna Szöke. 288 pp. 10 maps. 1964. 40s.*

Bonné, Alfred. State and Economics in the Middle East: A Society in Transition. *482 pp. 2nd (revised) edition 1955. (2nd Impression 1960.) 40s.*
Studies in Economic Development: with special reference to Conditions in the Under-developed Areas of Western Asia and India. *322 pp. 84 tables. 2nd edition 1960. 32s.*

Mayer, J. P. Political Thought in France from the Revolution to the Fifth Republic. *164 pp. 3rd edition (revised) 1961. 16s.*

CRIMINOLOGY

Ancel, Marc. Social Defence: A Modern Approach to Criminal Problems. *Foreword by Leon Radzinowicz. 240 pp. 1965. 32s.*

Cloward, Richard A., and Ohlin, Lloyd E. Delinquency and Opportunity: A Theory of Delinquent Gangs. *248 pp. 1961. 25s.*

Downes, David M. The Delinquent Solution. A Study in Subcultural Theory. *296 pp. 1966. 42s.*

Dunlop, A. B., and **McCabe, S.** Young Men in Detention Centres. *192 pp. 1965. 28s.*

Friedländer, Kate. The Psycho-Analytical Approach to Juvenile Delinquency: Theory, Case Studies, Treatment. *320 pp. 1947. (6th Impression 1967). 40s.*

Glueck, Sheldon and **Eleanor.** Family Environment and Delinquency. *With the statistical assistance of Rose W. Kneznek. 340 pp. 1962. (2nd Impression 1966.) 40s.*

Mannheim, Hermann. Comparative Criminology: a Text Book. *Two volumes. 442 pp. and 380 pp. 1965. (2nd Impression with corrections 1966.) 42s. a volume.*

Morris, Terence. The Criminal Area: A Study in Social Ecology. *Foreword by Hermann Mannheim. 232 pp. 25 tables. 4 maps. 1957. (2nd Impression 1966.) 28s.*

Morris, Terence and **Pauline,** assisted by **Barbara Barer.** Pentonville: A Sociological Study of an English Prison. *416 pp. 16 plates. 1963. 50s.*

Spencer, John C. Crime and the Services. *Foreword by Hermann Mannheim. 336 pp. 1954. 28s.*

Trasler, Gordon. The Explanation of Criminality. *144 pp. 1962. (2nd Impression 1967.) 20s.*

SOCIAL PSYCHOLOGY

Barbu, Zevedei. Problems of Historical Psychology. *248 pp. 1960. 25s.*

Blackburn, Julian. Psychology and the Social Pattern. *184 pp. 1945. (7th Impression 1964.) 16s.*

Fleming, C. M. Adolescence: Its Social Psychology: With an Introduction to recent findings from the fields of Anthropology, Physiology, Medicine, Psychometrics and Sociometry. *288 pp. 2nd edition (revised) 1963. (3rd Impression 1967.) 25s. Paper 12s. 6d.*

The Social Psychology of Education: An Introduction and Guide to Its Study. *136 pp. 2nd edition (revised) 1959. (4th Impression 1967.) 14s. Paper 7s. 6d.*

Homans, George C. The Human Group. *Foreword by Bernard DeVoto. Introduction by Robert K. Merton. 526 pp. 1951. (7th Impression 1968.) 35s.*

Social Behaviour: its Elementary Forms. *416 pp. 1961. (3rd Impression 1968.) 35s.*

Klein, Josephine. The Study of Groups. *226 pp. 31 figures. 5 tables. 1956. (5th Impression 1967.) 21s. Paper 9s. 6d.*

Linton, Ralph. The Cultural Background of Personality. *132 pp. 1947. (7th Impression 1968.) 18s.*

Mayo, Elton. The Social Problems of an Industrial Civilization. With an appendix on the Political Problem. *180 pp. 1949. (5th Impression 1966.) 25s.*

Ottaway, A. K. C. Learning Through Group Experience. *176 pp. 1966. (2nd Impression 1968.) 25s.*

Ridder, J. C. de. The Personality of the Urban African in South Africa. A Thematic Apperception Test Study. *196 pp. 12 plates. 1961. 25s.*

Rose, Arnold M. (Ed.). Human Behaviour and Social Processes: an Inter-actionist Approach. *Contributions by Arnold M. Rose, Ralph H. Turner, Anselm Strauss, Everett C. Hughes, E. Franklin Frazier, Howard S. Becker, et al. 696 pp. 1962. (2nd Impression 1968.) 70s.*

Smelser, Neil J. Theory of Collective Behaviour. *448 pp. 1962. (2nd Impression 1967.) 45s.*

Stephenson, Geoffrey M. The Development of Conscience. *128 pp. 1966. 25s.*

Young, Kimball. Handbook of Social Psychology. *658 pp. 16 figures. 10 tables. 2nd edition (revised) 1957. (3rd Impression 1963.) 40s.*

SOCIOLOGY OF THE FAMILY

Banks, J. A. Prosperity and Parenthood: A study of Family Planning among The Victorian Middle Classes. *262 pp. 1954. (3rd Impression 1968.) 28s.*

Bell, Colin R. Middle Class Families: Social and Geographical Mobility. *224 pp. 1969. 35s.*

Burton, Lindy. Vulnerable Children. *272 pp. 1968. 35s.*

Gavron, Hannah. The Captive Wife: Conflicts of Housebound Mothers. *190 pp. 1966. (2nd Impression 1966.) 25s.*

Klein, Josephine. Samples from English Cultures. *1965. (2nd Impression 1967.)*
  1. Three Preliminary Studies and Aspects of Adult Life in England. *447 pp. 50s.*
  2. Child-Rearing Practices and Index. *247 pp. 35s.*

Klein, Viola. Britain's Married Women Workers. *180 pp. 1965. (2nd Impression 1968.) 28s.*

McWhinnie, Alexina M. Adopted Children. How They Grow Up. *304 pp. 1967. (2nd Impression 1968.) 42s.*

Myrdal, Alva and **Klein, Viola.** Women's Two Roles: Home and Work. *238 pp. 27 tables. 1956. Revised Edition 1967. 30s. Paper 15s.*

Parsons, Talcott and **Bales, Robert F.** Family: Socialization and Interaction Process. *In collaboration with James Olds, Morris Zelditch and Philip E. Slater. 456 pp. 50 figures and tables. 1956. (3rd Impression 1968.) 45s.*

Schücking, L. L. The Puritan Family. *Translated from the German by Brian Battershaw. 212 pp. 1969. About 42s.*

7

THE SOCIAL SERVICES

Forder, R. A. (Ed.). Penelope Hall's Social Services of Modern England. *288 pp. 1969. 35s.*

George, Victor. Social Security: Beveridge and After. *258 pp. 1968. 35s.*

Goetschius, George W. Working with Community Groups. *256 pp. 1969. 35s.*

Goetschius, George W. and **Tash, Joan.** Working with Unattached Youth. *416 pp. 1967. (2nd Impression 1968.) 40s.*

Hall, M. P., and **Howes, I. V.** The Church in Social Work. A Study of Moral Welfare Work undertaken by the Church of England. *320 pp. 1965. 35s.*

Heywood, Jean S. Children in Care: the Development of the Service for the Deprived Child. *264 pp. 2nd edition (revised) 1965. (2nd Impression 1966.) 32s.*

An Introduction to Teaching Casework Skills. *190 pp. 1964. 28s.*

Jones, Kathleen. Lunacy, Law and Conscience, 1744-1845: the Social History of the Care of the Insane. *268 pp. 1955. 25s.*

Mental Health and Social Policy, 1845-1959. *264 pp. 1960. (2nd Impression 1967.) 32s.*

Jones, Kathleen and **Sidebotham, Roy.** Mental Hospitals at Work. *220 pp. 1962. 30s.*

Kastell, Jean. Casework in Child Care. *Foreword by M. Brooke Willis. 320 pp. 1962. 35s.*

Morris, Pauline. Put Away: A Sociological Study of Institutions for the Mentally Retarded. *Approx. 288 pp. 1969. About 50s.*

Nokes, P. L. The Professional Task in Welfare Practice. *152 pp. 1967. 28s.*

Rooff, Madeline. Voluntary Societies and Social Policy. *350 pp. 15 tables. 1957. 35s.*

Timms, Noel. Psychiatric Social Work in Great Britain (1939-1962). *280 pp. 1964. 32s.*

Social Casework: Principles and Practice. *256 pp. 1964. (2nd Impression 1966.) 25s. Paper 15s.*

Trasler, Gordon. In Place of Parents: A Study in Foster Care. *272 pp. 1960. (2nd Impression 1966.) 30s.*

Young, A. F., and **Ashton, E. T.** British Social Work in the Nineteenth Century. *288 pp. 1956. (2nd Impression 1963.) 28s.*

Young, A. F. Social Services in British Industry. *272 pp. 1968. 40s.*

SOCIOLOGY OF EDUCATION

Banks, Olive. Parity and Prestige in English Secondary Education: a Study in Educational Sociology. *272 pp. 1955. (2nd Impression 1963.) 32s.*

Bentwich, Joseph. Education in Israel. *224 pp. 8 pp. plates. 1965. 24s.*

Blyth, W. A. L. English Primary Education. A Sociological Description. *1965. Revised edition 1967.*

1. Schools. *232 pp. 30s. Paper 12s. 6d.*
2. Background. *168 pp. 25s. Paper 10s. 6d.*

Collier, K. G. The Social Purposes of Education: Personal and Social Values in Education. *268 pp. 1959. (3rd Impression 1965.) 21s.*

Dale, R. R., and **Griffith, S.** Down Stream: Failure in the Grammar School. *108 pp. 1965. 20s.*

Dore, R. P. Education in Tokugawa Japan. *356 pp. 9 pp. plates. 1965. 35s.*

Edmonds, E. L. The School Inspector. *Foreword by Sir William Alexander. 214 pp. 1962. 28s.*

Evans, K. M. Sociometry and Education. *158 pp. 1962. (2nd Impression 1966.) 18s.*

Foster, P. J. Education and Social Change in Ghana. *336 pp. 3 maps. 1965. (2nd Impression 1967.) 36s.*

Fraser, W. R. Education and Society in Modern France. *150 pp. 1963. (2nd Impression 1968.) 25s.*

Hans, Nicholas. New Trends in Education in the Eighteenth Century. *278 pp. 19 tables. 1951. (2nd Impression 1966.) 30s.*
Comparative Education: A Study of Educational Factors and Traditions. *360 pp. 3rd (revised) edition 1958. (4th Impression 1967.) 25s. Paper 12s. 6d.*

Hargreaves, David. Social Relations in a Secondary School. *240 pp. 1967. (2nd Impression 1968.) 32s.*

Holmes, Brian. Problems in Education. A Comparative Approach. *336 pp. 1965. (2nd Impression 1967.) 32s.*

Mannheim, Karl and **Stewart, W. A. C.** An Introduction to the Sociology of Education. *206 pp. 1962. (2nd Impression 1965.) 21s.*

Morris, Raymond N. The Sixth Form and College Entrance. *231 pp. 1969. 40s.*

Musgrove, F. Youth and the Social Order. *176 pp. 1964. (2nd Impression 1968.) 25s. Paper 12s.*

Ortega y Gasset, José. Mission of the University. *Translated with an Introduction by Howard Lee Nostrand. 86 pp. 1946. (3rd Impression 1963.) 15s.*

Ottaway, A. K. C. Education and Society: An Introduction to the Sociology of Education. *With an Introduction by W. O. Lester Smith. 212 pp. Second edition (revised). 1962. (5th Impression 1968.) 18s. Paper 10s. 6d.*

Peers, Robert. Adult Education: A Comparative Study. *398 pp. 2nd edition 1959. (2nd Impression 1966.) 42s.*

Pritchard, D. G. Education and the Handicapped: 1760 to 1960. *258 pp. 1963. (2nd Impression 1966.) 35s.*

Richardson, Helen. Adolescent Girls in Approved Schools. *Approx. 360 pp. 1969. About 42s.*

Simon, Brian and **Joan** (Eds.). Educational Psychology in the U.S.S.R. *Introduction by Brian and Joan Simon. Translation by Joan Simon. Papers by D. N. Bogoiavlenski and N. A. Menchinskaia, D. B. Elkonin, E. A. Fleshner, Z. I. Kalmykova, G. S. Kostiuk, V. A. Krutetski, A. N. Leontiev, A. R. Luria, E. A. Milerian, R. G. Natadze, B. M. Teplov, L. S. Vygotski, L. V. Zankov. 296 pp. 1963. 40s.*

SOCIOLOGY OF CULTURE

Eppel, E. M., and M. Adolescents and Morality: A Study of some Moral Values and Dilemmas of Working Adolescents in the Context of a changing Climate of Opinion. *Foreword by W. J. H. Sprott. 268 pp. 39 tables. 1966. 30s.*

Fromm, Erich. The Fear of Freedom. *286 pp. 1942. (8th Impression 1960.) 25s. Paper 10s.*

The Sane Society. *400 pp. 1956. (4th Impression 1968.) 28s. Paper 14s.*

Mannheim, Karl. Diagnosis of Our Time: Wartime Essays of a Sociologist. *208 pp. 1943. (8th Impression 1966.) 21s.*

Essays on the Sociology of Culture. *Edited by Ernst Mannheim in co-operation with Paul Kecskemeti. Editorial Note by Adolph Lowe. 280 pp. 1956. (3rd Impression 1967.) 28s.*

Weber, Alfred. Farewell to European History: or The Conquest of Nihilism. *Translated from the German by R. F. C. Hull. 224 pp. 1947. 18s.*

SOCIOLOGY OF RELIGION

Argyle, Michael. Religious Behaviour. *224 pp. 8 figures. 41 tables. 1958. (4th Impression 1968.) 25s.*

Nelson, G. K. Spiritualism and Society. *313 pp. 1969. 42s.*

Stark, Werner. The Sociology of Religion. A Study of Christendom.
Volume I. Established Religion. *248 pp. 1966. 35s.*
Volume II. Sectarian Religion. *368 pp. 1967. 40s.*
Volume III. The Universal Church. *464 pp. 1967. 45s.*

Watt, W. Montgomery. Islam and the Integration of Society. *320 pp. 1961. (3rd Impression 1966.) 35s.*

SOCIOLOGY OF ART AND LITERATURE

Beljame, Alexandre. Men of Letters and the English Public in the Eighteenth Century: 1660-1744, Dryden, Addison, Pope. *Edited with an Introduction and Notes by Bonamy Dobrée. Translated by E. O. Lorimer. 532 pp. 1948. 32s.*

Misch, Georg. A History of Autobiography in Antiquity. *Translated by E. W. Dickes. 2 Volumes. Vol. 1, 364 pp., Vol. 2, 372 pp. 1950. 45s. the set.*

Schücking, L. L. The Sociology of Literary Taste. *112 pp. 2nd (revised) edition 1966. 18s.*

Silbermann, Alphons. The Sociology of Music. *Translated from the German by Corbet Stewart. 222 pp. 1963. 32s.*

SOCIOLOGY OF KNOWLEDGE

Mannheim, Karl. Essays on the Sociology of Knowledge. *Edited by Paul Kecskemeti. Editorial note by Adolph Lowe. 352 pp. 1952. (4th Impression 1967.) 35s.*

Stark, W. America: Ideal and Reality. The United States of 1776 in Contemporary Philosophy. *136 pp. 1947. 12s.*

The Sociology of Knowledge: An Essay in Aid of a Deeper Understanding of the History of Ideas. *384 pp. 1958. (3rd Impression 1967.) 36s.*

Montesquieu: Pioneer of the Sociology of Knowledge. *244 pp. 1960. 25s.*

URBAN SOCIOLOGY

Anderson, Nels. The Urban Community: A World Perspective. *532 pp. 1960. 35s.*

Ashworth, William. The Genesis of Modern British Town Planning: A Study in Economic and Social History of the Nineteenth and Twentieth Centuries. *288 pp. 1954. (3rd Impression 1968.) 32s.*

Bracey, Howard. Neighbours: On New Estates and Subdivisions in England and U.S.A. *220 pp. 1964. 28s.*

Cullingworth, J. B. Housing Needs and Planning Policy: A Restatement of the Problems of Housing Need and "Overspill" in England and Wales. *232 pp. 44 tables. 8 maps. 1960. (2nd Impression 1966.) 28s.*

Dickinson, Robert E. City and Region: A Geographical Interpretation. *608 pp. 125 figures. 1964. (5th Impression 1967.) 60s.*

The West European City: A Geographical Interpretation. *600 pp. 129 maps. 29 plates. 2nd edition 1962. (3rd Impression 1968.) 55s.*

The City Region in Western Europe. *320 pp. Maps. 1967. 30s. Paper 14s.*

Jackson, Brian. Working Class Community: Some General Notions raised by a Series of Studies in Northern England. *192 pp. 1968. (2nd Impression 1968.) 25s.*

Jennings, Hilda. Societies in the Making: a Study of Development and Redevelopment within a County Borough. *Foreword by D. A. Clark. 286 pp. 1962. (2nd Impression 1967.) 32s.*

Kerr, Madeline. The People of Ship Street. *240 pp. 1958. 28s.*

Mann, P. H. An Approach to Urban Sociology. *240 pp. 1965. (2nd Impression 1968.) 30s.*

Morris, R. N., and **Mogey, J.** The Sociology of Housing. Studies at Berinsfield. *232 pp. 4 pp. plates. 1965. 42s.*

Rosser, C., and **Harris, C.** The Family and Social Change. A Study of Family and Kinship in a South Wales Town. *352 pp. 8 maps. 1965. (2nd Impression 1968.) 45s.*

RURAL SOCIOLOGY

Chambers, R. J. H. Settlement Schemes in Africa: A Selective Study. *Approx. 268 pp. 1969. About 50s.*

Haswell, M. R. The Economics of Development in Village India. *120 pp. 1967. 21s.*

11

Littlejohn, James. Westrigg: the Sociology of a Cheviot Parish. *172 pp. 5 figures. 1963. 25s.*

Williams, W. M. The Country Craftsman: A Study of Some Rural Crafts and the Rural Industries Organization in England. *248 pp. 9 figures. 1958. 25s.* (*Dartington Hall Studies in Rural Sociology.*)
The Sociology of an English Village: Gosforth. *272 pp. 12 figures. 13 tables. 1956.* (*3rd Impression 1964.*) *25s.*

SOCIOLOGY OF MIGRATION

Humphreys, Alexander J. New Dubliners: Urbanization and the Irish Family. *Foreword by George C. Homans. 304 pp. 1966. 40s.*

SOCIOLOGY OF INDUSTRY AND DISTRIBUTION

Anderson, Nels. Work and Leisure. *280 pp. 1961. 28s.*

Blau, Peter M., and **Scott, W. Richard.** Formal Organizations: a Comparative approach. *Introduction and Additional Bibliography by J. H. Smith. 326 pp. 1963.* (*4th Impression 1969.*) *35s. Paper 15s.*

Eldridge, J. E. T. Industrial Disputes. Essays in the Sociology of Industrial Relations. *288 pp. 1968. 40s.*

Hollowell, Peter G. The Lorry Driver. *272 pp. 1968. 42s.*

Jefferys, Margot, with the assistance of Winifred Moss. Mobility in the Labour Market: Employment Changes in Battersea and Dagenham. *Preface by Barbara Wootton. 186 pp. 51 tables. 1954. 15s.*

Levy, A. B. Private Corporations and Their Control. *Two Volumes. Vol. 1, 464 pp., Vol. 2, 432 pp. 1950. 80s. the set.*

Liepmann, Kate. Apprenticeship: An Enquiry into its Adequacy under Modern Conditions. *Foreword by H. D. Dickinson. 232 pp. 6 tables. 1960.* (*2nd Impression 1960.*) *23s.*

Millerson, Geoffrey. The Qualifying Associations: a Study in Professionalization. *320 pp. 1964. 42s.*

Smelser, Neil J. Social Change in the Industrial Revolution: An Application of Theory to the Lancashire Cotton Industry, 1770-1840. *468 pp. 12 figures. 14 tables. 1959.* (*2nd Impression 1960.*) *50s.*

Williams, Gertrude. Recruitment to Skilled Trades. *240 pp. 1957. 23s.*

Young, A. F. Industrial Injuries Insurance: an Examination of British Policy. *192 pp. 1964. 30s.*

ANTHROPOLOGY

Ammar, Hamed. Growing up in an Egyptian Village: Silwa, Province of Aswan. *336 pp. 1954.* (*2nd Impression 1966.*) *35s.*

Crook, David and **Isabel.** Revolution in a Chinese Village: Ten Mile Inn. *230 pp. 8 plates. 1 map. 1959.* (*2nd Impression 1968.*) *21s.*
The First Years of Yangyi Commune. *302 pp. 12 plates. 1966. 42s.*

12

Dickie-Clark, H. F. The Marginal Situation. A Sociological Study of a Coloured Group. *236 pp. 1966. 40s.*

Dube, S. C. Indian Village. *Foreword by Morris Edward Opler. 276 pp. 4 plates. 1955. (5th Impression 1965.) 25s.*
India's Changing Villages: Human Factors in Community Development. *260 pp. 8 plates. 1 map. 1958. (3rd Impression 1963.) 25s.*

Firth, Raymond. Malay Fishermen. Their Peasant Economy. *420 pp. 17 pp. plates. 2nd edition revised and enlarged 1966. (2nd Impression 1968.) 55s.*

Gulliver, P. H. The Family Herds. A Study of two Pastoral Tribes in East Africa, The Jie and Turkana. *304 pp. 4 plates. 19 figures. 1955. (2nd Impression with new preface and bibliography 1966.) 35s.*
Social Control in an African Society: a Study of the Arusha, Agricultural Masai of Northern Tanganyika. *320 pp. 8 plates. 10 figures. 1963. (2nd Impression 1968.) 42s.*

Ishwaran, K. Shivapur. A South Indian Village. *216 pp. 1968. 35s.*
Tradition and Economy in Village India: An Interactionist Approach. *Foreword by Conrad Arensburg. 176 pp. 1966. (2nd Impression 1968.) 25s.*

Jarvie, Ian C. The Revolution in Anthropology. *268 pp. 1964. (2nd Impression 1967.) 40s.*

Jarvie, Ian C. and Agassi, Joseph. Hong Kong. A Society in Transition. *396 pp. Illustrated with plates and maps. 1968. 56s.*

Little, Kenneth L. Mende of Sierra Leone. *308 pp. and folder. 1951. Revised edition 1967. 63s.*

Lowie, Professor Robert H. Social Organization. *494 pp. 1950. (4th Impression 1966.) 50s.*

Mayer, Adrian C. Caste and Kinship in Central India: A Village and its Region. *328 pp. 16 plates. 15 figures. 16 tables. 1960. (2nd Impression 1965.) 35s.*
Peasants in the Pacific: A Study of Fiji Indian Rural Society. *232 pp. 16 plates. 10 figures. 14 tables. 1961. 35s.*

Smith, Raymond T. The Negro Family in British Guiana: Family Structure and Social Status in the Villages. *With a Foreword by Meyer Fortes. 314 pp. 8 plates. 1 figure. 4 maps. 1956. (2nd Impression 1965.) 35s.*

DOCUMENTARY

Meek, Dorothea L. (Ed.). Soviet Youth: Some Achievements and Problems. *Excerpts from the Soviet Press, translated by the editor. 280 pp. 1957. 28s.*

Schlesinger, Rudolf (Ed.). Changing Attitudes in Soviet Russia.
2. The Nationalities Problem and Soviet Administration. Selected Readings on the Development of Soviet Nationalities Policies. *Introduced by the editor. Translated by W. W. Gottlieb. 324 pp. 1956. 30s.*

Reports of the Institute of Community Studies

(*Demy 8vo.*)

Cartwright, Ann. Human Relations and Hospital Care. *272 pp. 1964. 30s.*

Patients and their Doctors. A Study of General Practice. *304 pp. 1967. 40s.*

Jackson, Brian. Streaming: an Education System in Miniature. *168 pp. 1964. (2nd Impression 1966.) 21s. Paper 10s.*

Jackson, Brian and **Marsden, Dennis.** Education and the Working Class: Some General Themes raised by a Study of 88 Working-class Children in a Northern Industrial City. *268 pp. 2 folders. 1962. (4th Impression 1968.) 32s.*

Marris, Peter. Widows and their Families. *Foreword by Dr. John Bowlby. 184 pp. 18 tables. Statistical Summary. 1958. 18s.*
Family and Social Change in an African City. A Study of Rehousing in Lagos. *196 pp. 1 map. 4 plates. 53 tables. 1961. (2nd Impression 1966.) 30s.*
The Experience of Higher Education. *232 pp. 27 tables. 1964. 25s.*

Marris, Peter and **Rein, Martin.** Dilemmas of Social Reform. Poverty and Community Action in the United States. *256 pp. 1967. 35s.*

Mills, Enid. Living with Mental Illness: a Study in East London. *Foreword by Morris Carstairs. 196 pp. 1962. 28s.*

Runciman, W. G. Relative Deprivation and Social Justice. A Study of Attitudes to Social Inequality in Twentieth Century England. *352 pp. 1966. (2nd Impression 1967.) 40s.*

Townsend, Peter. The Family Life of Old People: An Inquiry in East London. *Foreword by J. H. Sheldon. 300 pp. 3 figures. 63 tables. 1957. (3rd Impression 1967.) 30s.*

Willmott, Peter. Adolescent Boys in East London. *230 pp. 1966. 30s.*
The Evolution of a Community: a study of Dagenham after forty years. *168 pp. 2 maps. 1963. 21s.*

Willmott, Peter and **Young, Michael.** Family and Class in a London Suburb. *202 pp. 47 tables. 1960. (4th Impression 1968.) 25s.*

Young, Michael. Innovation and Research in Education. *192 pp. 1965. 25s. Paper 12s. 6d.*

Young, Michael and **McGeeney, Patrick.** Learning Begins at Home. A Study of a Junior School and its Parents. *About 128 pp. 1968. 21s. Paper 14s.*

Young, Michael and **Willmott, Peter.** Family and Kinship in East London. *Foreword by Richard M. Titmuss. 252 pp. 39 tables. 1957. (3rd Impression 1965.) 28s.*

The British Journal of Sociology. *Edited by Terence P. Morris. Vol. 1, No. 1, March 1950 and Quarterly. Roy. 8vo., £3 annually, 15s. a number, post free. (Vols. 1-18, £8 each. Individual parts £2 10s.*

All prices are net and subject to alteration without notice

15

1268 H.B.